Refined

By Grace

Calvary

By Regina D. Thomas

Refined By Grace Calvary

ISBN: 978-0692766415

Edited by Asoral

All scriptures are taken from the King James Version of the Bible unless otherwise stated. Some of the commentaries were taken from the PC Study Bible 3.1 version for Windows. Some of the comments from Barnes' notes were paraphrased. The Greek and Hebrew definitions: were taken from the Strong's Concordance, which may also have some paraphrasing. Other definitions were taken from the Ultimate Talking Dictionary. Comments were made from authors of other materials on the subject. No notes were taken from them. Summary was taken from: Microsoft Word.

This book was printed in the United States of America.
To order additional copies of this book, contact:
www.restorativehopeministry.org
treginapma@aol.com
803 834 3341

Table of Contents

Dedication

This book is to all believers washed in the blood, who
are true followers (disciples) aspiring to move from
the laying of foundation of repentance of dead works
to a level of spiritual maturity, a way of perfection in
the things of Christ, fulfilling purpose.

Acknowledgements

To my husband James, children Tamara, Nilka, James Jr. and Neysa. To all of my grandchildren: Xenia, Faaifo, Isiah, Amoni, and Zari Milan. My love to all of my brothers and sisters, and to Irina my daughter in the faith. Thank you for your help Earline. You saved the day, once again.

Introduction

Seeing the cross as the only object of faith makes the journey easier. It all started and ends at Calvary. We must never lose sight of the cross because it is the only thing that makes the difference in whether we have eternal life or not. This does not mean there will be no problems, it only gives us appreciation, and a better life in Christ as the Holy Spirit leads us.

Saved by Grace Ephesians 2:8

Grace allows us to access the kingdom and everything in it as heirs of the promise as, sons.

What does grace do?

Grace is a gift we take through faith and faith is obtained by staying in the Word.

Grace gives us access to the Father, it is a person. Grace does not do things for us it opens the door so we can utilize our faith and receive all that grace provides. It is a vehicle, it is a key that opens the door to the Father. (Revelation3:20)

This speaks to the believer saying, "Behold I stand at your hearts door knocking, if anyone hears my voice and ask me to come in. I will come into him and will supp with him and he with me."

Grace gives the ability to be refined and perfected as vessels fit for the master's use.

Grace is instant and yet continues for a believer that has repented.

Refined, (adjective): Is continuously removing impurities and unwanted elements. It is a process. Life is a journey, as one walking up the straight and narrow path. It's never a smooth path, but one filled with oppositions, discouragements, disappointments, sickness and issues of life. Therefore, we're not thanking Him for the issues, rather we give thanks while we are going through them.

One of our greatest weapons is our Praise, the fruit of our lips giving thanks as we enjoy the benefits he gives such as, Joy, Peace and Forgiveness.

To the believer these issues only serve as opportunity, giving way to all we need. It prepares us for a greater event, His return. Without grace this will not be possible. It is through the refining process that prepares us to meet Him.

Grace keeps us cultured and elegant in appearance.

Discuss the Garments:
Grace gives us the right to the right-apparel.
- Dressed with the Priestly Robe, High Priest Robe (Aaron and his sons) Exodus 28.

- Dressed with the Robe of Righteousness (Isiah 61:10).
- Dressed with the Garments of Salvation (Isiah 61:10).
- Dressed with the whole Armor of God (Ephesians 6:10).
- Dressed as The Bride of Christ prepared for her Bridegroom (Revelation 21:1).
- Dressed with the Garment of Praise (Isiah 61:3).
- Dressed with Love and dressed with the overcomer's garments as in the book of Revelation. These are just a few to mention.

As believers in Christ we wear different garments; sacred garments that bring dignity and honor to our God. When we serve as priest, we serve in ministry before the Lord in consecration with priestly garments. (Exodus 28, 29)

It is important that we seek to understand and acknowledge the supernatural finish work of Calvary, then begin to enjoy the benefits.

Being changed and refined through the process must be a continuous abiding on your part. It will manifest itself in restfulness and shows your steadfastness and obedience.

Preface

All believers will benefit from the contents written herein, the mature as well as the immature. You will be amazed to know that there are many, who are unaware of the fact that God has a plan and purpose for each believer, including themselves. I am not talking about reciting it, but true knowledge in their heart a deep conviction of the Spirit. Proclaiming the gospel of the Kingdom and the Name of Jesus is for all who are redeemed.

From the beginning of mankind we see: through one man's disobedience the relationship was affected and severed. Fellowship with the Creator was broken because of sin.

Man found himself in a place where he needed to be reconciled to God. He had to acknowledge the importance of his need for a Savior or mediator, found only in the person of Jesus Christ the righteous through repentance.

Because of the sin of one man, Adam, death included all under the penalty of sin. Whereby humanity took on the nature of sin.

As a means of reconciling man back to himself, Jehovah instituted the system of sacrifice for the people. Now the High-Priest could make atonement for the sin of the people once a year with the blood of bulls and goats. This was only a temporary sacrifice to satisfy Jehovah. Without the shedding of blood there is no remission of sin the scriptures say.

This temporary means instituted by God was acceptable. However, it took more than the blood of bullocks and goats. Jesus shed his blood once and for all as a more perfect sacrifice.

You will also discover what it will take for a true disciple to be back in good standing with God. What is required to walk fellowship and friendship with Him again, only through the finished work of the Cross.

It is impossible to grow spiritually without implementing the principles of the Word of God. It's a process. We must learn how to live by the principles of the Word, and this is how we are transformed, along with the Word we need the how to. The Bible says, "My people are destroyed from lack of knowledge". (Hosea 4:6 KJV). Without it, no one can do what he or she has no knowledge of. Jesus understood this and went about making disciples and teaching them. We see this with the "Sermon on the Mount" found in Mathew, chapters five, six and seven. Each believer is instructed to do the same. "Someone once said a disciple is not born but made," I say through teaching as well through his or her desire, to obey the commands of the word.

We will also deal with the unpopular subject of sin. There is much to be said concerning the habitual practice of sin, which usually culminates in a sense of estrangement or alienation and disunion from God and things related to Him.

The Word teaches us that, God never leaves us. We move out and away from Him.

In this book you will have a better understanding of the amazing difference the death and resurrection of Jesus made. Grace gave us the ability through faith. His grace provided us with the freedom of not having to be controlled by the old nature. Now we can resist the flesh and avoid succumbing to the activity of sin through knowledge and the power of the Holy Spirit. We no longer have to be slaves to the Devil nor our sinful nature.

Jesus died a cruel death on the cross of Calvary for our sin, and to redeem us from the penalty of the curse we are under. His death also obtained the victory over death and hell, rescuing us from a life once lost in sin, whereby we were separated from a loving Father. Now by the power of his resurrection we receive grace, by which we can live a transformed life through Jesus Christ.

My intent is that through the scriptures you encounter here, it will be beneficial with its incredible and simplified manner. May it provide you with insight into the glorious gospel of Jesus Christ. May you experience a real encounter with the God of the Bible.

I'm proud to recommend this book as a helpful tool to help you grow. It can be used in women's group, Bible study or extracurricular reading. I'm convinced, anyone who can read will be able to comprehend what is written therein. Consider the words of the patriarch Job, a perfect and upright man. One that feared God and eschewed evil. He stated in (Job 32:8 KJV), "But there is a spirit in man: and the inspiration of the Almighty giveth them understanding. My prayer is: that you will be enlightened.

Another translation states it this way, "But there is a spirit in man, and the breath of the Almighty gives him understanding". Wherefore, I pray you also will get spiritual understanding from the Lord as you read it prayerfully allowing the Holy Spirit to speak to your heart as you challenge yourself to obey. In essence the verse is saying that primarily man's understanding comes from the Spirit of God within. We receive understanding through the impartation and quickening of the Holy Spirit. I find that during prayer and meditation, while I commune with the Lord, is most commonly when things are revealed to me.

I make it a practice to research the Word to ensure accuracy and to clear up any uncertainty I encounter. I like to be sure that my interpretation or revelation which I believed was of the Lord, (Rhema word), does not violate the meaning of the Scripture, nor change it in any fashion. Hopefully some clarity will be provided to assist you in your walk.

Some areas I will endeavor to cover are as follows: Sin, Atonement, Grace, Mercy and The Cross among other subjects.

There is also a section throughout the book for discussion, questions and answers.

What is sin?
Where did it originate?
How does God view it?

What has God said concerning it? How it affects our relationship to him and others.

We will also discover the consequence for its habitual practice, how it hinders and   stagnates us in our walk and relationship with your God.

Benefits and privileges:

As the Redeemed of the Lord, there are expectations of obedience on our part, in order for us to receive the benefits promised. God's promises are conditional. This is not talking about the unmerited favor of God's Saving grace. Grace is free and it is the ability to access God through faith. Jesus paid the price to purchase that for us. It is unmerited and we did not have to do anything or participate in that activity. However in order for it to benefit us we must take hold of it by faith. We will also cover the Divine Favor of God which comes through our obedience, it is also conditional and only available to believers who are in Christ.

Open your mind and challenge yourself to search the Scriptures. Seek The Father for clarity on this subject. It is one that needs comprehension because perhaps of:

      a) previous teaching,

      b) personal agendas,

      c) powers of darkness.

God is clear we are not. Challenge yourself to inquire of Him.

God also expects us to extend grace to each other. We will learn to give freely what we ourselves have received. The metaphors and allegories are used to make it easier for the reader to understand the message.

My prayer is that it may whet your appetite for the things of God. I pray it challenges you to seek more of Him. You will allow him to speak to you by reading his Word. Obey God. Move out of your comfort zone, whatever it may be. Go on to maturity in Christ. I will assure you, your life will be fruitful and you will experience much increase as you walk with Him in truth.

Chapter 1
Justified Through the Cross

By way of a special introduction, I'll attempt to encapsulate my thoughts in this book. In it I stress the need for having some kind of basic knowledge of the Bible. You can do this yourself by taking a simple course or with your Bible Study group. It will be pivotal in launching you into a dimension you will not regret. You will discover how beneficial it is to your personal walk, as well as with helping others in their walk.

It will provide insight and understanding of your position in the plan of God for your life as a believer. It will take you from where you are to where you are designed to go faster, with knowledge. You will learn how to apply the principles of the Word through faith, using His wisdom. However, this does not mean you have arrived, neither are you perfect. By no means. I am merely saying it's worth the drive! As with any profession. Be it carpentry, medical, auto mechanic, education, or business, you need specific education in order to be effectual. Some sort of basic instruction is required. Even so, the believer as well, needs to be equipped with proper tools to execute the business of The Kingdom. This provides The Holy Spirit something to work with, after all He is the teacher and guide. Likewise we also have a vocation. We must also specialize in order to be proficient at what we are called to do.

Empower yourself with the Scriptures by acquainting yourself with the theme and books of the Bible. Know how they are divided and what each one is about.

It may be helpful for you to educate yourself on a brief overview of the entire Bible to get a better picture.

It's imperative you know who you are in Him, and your inheritance. Know what is expected of you and study the scriptures to help you get there. Notice I did not say read, but study.

It is almost impossible to do the Will without knowing the Creator, who wrote it. It will enable you to be confident of your uniqueness, and His ultimate purpose for fearfully and wonderfully crafting you.

You need to know; the who, what, when and where of the Bible. It is for you, to equip you so that you may go and tell others, and they too, may also go and tell others, and Gods family will grow.

We must know how to pray and who we are praying to. Be intentional about getting prayers answered by faith.

I would say to you, don't just read the Bible, but know who and what you are looking for in the

Bible. Learn to observe what is said, then interpret it by asking yourself, "What is God saying to me?" then put it into practice. You do not know it until you begin to do it. It is a process as you grow in grace.

Finally, study to show yourself approved and attractive to God. He will be attracted to you and will bless you according to Deuteronomy 28.

We glean more when we approach the Bible looking back from the beginning, since that's where it all started. The Old Testament was mostly about his coming while the New Testament announces his arrival.

As we follow the teachings we will see a pattern, giving us some basic understanding of why and how the Bible was written. I assure you the journey will be fuller, and your joy richer. It will show you what He came to do, and what that can do for your life as a believer.

Since the fall of man, we see His transcending love throughout the ages. God has endeavored to reach every man, woman, boy and girl through the preaching of the gospel and this is recorded. The way He has crossed every racial and cultural barrier is also recorded for our benefit. This record details hoe He is reaching every nation, tribe and tongue with the gospel, proclaiming his love. John 3:16 the Scripture declares, "For God so love the world He gave his only begotten Son." Imagine this: "Even while we were yet in our sins, Christ died for us." and not for us only, but for the entire world." (Romans 5:8 paraphrased). Thank God he does not deal with us according to our sins or no one would be saved.

Because of His grace, righteousness was imputed unto us, being in Christ, we are declared justified by faith. In (Romans 5:1 TLB) we read, "Because we have been made right based on what Jesus did, and not what we ourselves have done. We have peace with God." Thank God, through Jesus we now have a better covenant, obtained for us through the shed blood of Jesus on Calvary's cross.

I pray at the conclusion of your reading you will have a complete understanding of how much God loves you, and wants to be close to you. How he desires to change your life.

He wants you to experience Him in a new and living way, then go and make disciples. His desire is that   unbelievers will find comfort in Him, through your witness. Isaiah 40:1 says, "Comfort ye, comfort ye my people." When you read the Word you will understand how valuable you are to the Kingdom and getting the work done bringing the Word of comfort. You are his delegated voice and hands to the world, and to Gods people as well. It is of the utmost importance to study and read the Word in order for us to understand the magnitude of our assignment.

Being aware of what Christ accomplished on the cross, as you begin to trust Him, your joy will be fulfilled. You will now be privileged to pursue a deep relationship and friendship with your Creator. Don't just make him Savior, make him Lord as you personalize the Word and take heed to it. That same Word will become more and more profitable unto you as well, while you become more confident, you will be better able to serve those who are downtrodden in spirit. This will show them that everything they need is in the cross.

Benefits of salvation:

These are some of the benefits that accompany our salvation: healing, deliverance, courage, understanding, compassion, confidence, faith, restoration, favor, prosperity and much more.

These promises are to every believer after receiving Christ. I challenge you to inquire, seek more understanding concerning your benefits as a Kingdom dweller. We have an inheritance in Him now, as well as, in the world to come. Because we are heirs, and joint heirs of all of his promises of riches in glory. We are partakers of a better Covenant, as overcomers and soldiers of the cross. We are also assets to the kingdom of God, we are his prize possession.

As an Evangelist, in my travels, I get to see the needs of the people. I earnestly pray and petition the Lord for answers. This is something, I certainly did not have, but I knew One who did.

I remember an incident during a revival in one of the mission fields. The pastor asked the team to pray, in private, for a little girl who was about nine (9) years old at the time. She was being abused sexually by older men who would give her literally small change, a quarter or so. She was a pretty little girl. You could tell her innocent mind was already warped and marred by sin. Her mother was a believer. It was obvious she was very broken in her spirit. She didn't know what else to do with her disobedience. The little girl had no concept of what was happening to her. I imagine, in her innocence as a little girl being used in this way she wasn't able to perceive the consequence or danger of it.

It was painful to process that horrendous activity in my mind. We prayed earnestly believing on Jesus to step into the situation and minister to her.

We talked to her mainly about how precious she was to the Father who loved her. We told her how beautiful God saw her and would forgive her if she asked him to. We also encouraged her not to allow men to do evil things to her. To tell her mother who would protect her and to listen and obey her mother when she spoke. She had gotten so many spankings none of which helped according to her mother. That beautiful little girl's heart seemed so hardened, she just stared at each of our faces. There was no expression or fear; she said not a word to us. This moved me to righteous indignation to no end, to see what the enemy had done. I became angry at that liar. After all this, we were loving on her. I did not want to scare her so I was hugging and cuddling her in my arms.

We all gently prayed and petitioned God for her salvation and deliverance. I can still recall how we interceded and cried out to God on her behalf. Finally she was broken and tears began to flow from her beautiful eyes. We knew the Holy Spirit was at work. After ministering to her we encouraged her to hug her mother. We really praised Jesus that day for answering our prayers. It was an experience I will never forget. It took much prayer to get to her heart. How I would love to know what became of that little girl and her mother. I am always moving about, therefore I have not gone back to that area. Yet I continue to pray for that little girl whenever the thought crosses my mind. There are so many similar stories of little children that it would take too much time to tell them all.

My spirit often cries out whenever I encounter these feelings of inadequacy. I am challenged to seek The Lord more earnestly. There are times the burden upon my heart seemed to intensify, while questions surge through my mind and all I can do is reach out to

God, seeking to find his face. It causes me to recognize my need to understand the assignment entrusted to me. I ask myself the question again, and again: "What do I have to offer to these people?" Finally it dawned on me. It absolutely has nothing to do with me or my feelings. I was just a vessel chosen to be used for His glory. "Faithful was he who called me, and would complete that which he has called me to do." I realized, all I needed to do was obey and follow His leading. I have seen Him work miracle after miracle amongst the people time and time again.

He cannot lie. He has the power to perform all He has promised. He would never fail or go back on his word.

The Gospel Is Simple:
The simplicity of the gospel is enough to change lives. I have come to realize it is not by might nor by power, but by the Spirit of the Lord. He alone has the power to influence them through the preached Word. If they would only believe on this Jesus I was presenting to them, they could be saved. It suddenly dawned on me, that as a delegate of the Kingdom, I played a vital role in their salvation. I was chosen to represent Him. I knew he had a plan and wanted to do great things because of his great love for them.

I remember when my pastor taught on the *"Grace Gifts"* from the book written by Dr. Lim. It was such an insightful teaching. Learning those concepts helped me tremendously and broadened my understanding. I am more informed on the subject, I am also more confident in the way I now view my purpose and position in ministry. Besides that, my motivation has increased. I know, I'm in the place God would have me to be in with Him. He is (El berit), the God I'm in covenant with, who never breaks it. It is good to know you are in the place God expects you to be in, (Adam where are you?) I realize I am His ambassador sent to represent Him to those who once knew Him and are fallen away. I am to present Him to those who have never met him.

(1Timothy 1:12). "I thank Christ Jesus our Lord, who has given me strength, that he considered me faithful, appointing me to his service." To know that God has a need for me is reassuring. It brings me great joy and comfort. First and foremost I acknowledge him as my Lord, my Shepherd, Redeemer and friend. He is the manager of my soul. He has enabled and given me the strength needed to perform the task. Not only has he carefully thought, weighed, and judged me, but he has found me capable of performing the job. He has appointed and assigned me as a part of his team for service. I am convinced, this is the way God wants to feel about all of his children. He needs us. He is looking for soldiers he can count on. Will you be accounted worthy, as to be assigned by Christ today?

I realized many had heard the gospel over and over, but had not experienced any change or transformation in their life. I am glad to be one of many, who are sent to sow, or water the seed until he deems fit to give the increase. I had become a Kingdom connection between Him and the people. Not that I was so special, I was just available. And because of my readiness and obedience, I've been privileged to see many souls taken out of darkness and translated into the kingdom of light. Every believer is expected to be found faithful and become a Kingdom connector. It is not about us. It is about the people at the bottom of the mountain, those whom we are sent to serve. Those of the world of whom we once were. We are extension of his hands. Imagine yourself, as being the hands of the God of the whole earth. This revelation has impacted me so that, suddenly I understood the awesome responsibility placed upon me as an evangelist sent by God to gather his people.

I am fully persuaded I had been called to be a part of the five-fold ministry according to Ephesians 4:11. This calling was not by the will of men, but by the will of God.

The grace of God:

What is Grace?
Grace is the undeserved or unmeritted favor of God. As it relates to salvation, nothing is required on

our part, it is solely based on what Jesus did for us. It is a free gift.

In order to get its full understanding it is important that we keep this word in context, meaning with the text. Further in the book we will look at some other examples based on Scripture of how it is used based on contents in the context. What it relates to when it is used in that context.

Grace is a person (Jesus),
Grace is an action, such as kindness.

Grace can be demonstrated in your daily life according to the scriptures, having grace towards each other, being Christ like in all we do.

Because this is a very misunderstood subject, I believe it is necessary for all believers to get some basic understanding. Seek the Holy Spirit for His interpretation. Again, you do not have to participate by doing any works in order to experience grace. It is demonstrated in various ways and at different times. Even in the Old Testament. Although we do not see the word grace there it has always been present. It is Jesus! Promised throughout the Scriptures as: Jesus is coming and revealed to us in the New Testament saying, "Jesus the Messiah is here." He came with purpose as was outlined in the OT (Old Testament). And manifested with a fulfillment of that promise in the NT (New Testament). Bringing salvation, and

(Resurrection power) through His death on the cross, giving life and access to The Kingdom and all who would receive Him. God in his wisdom and sovereignty had predestined before the foundation, the coming of His Son Jesus. It would all be done in Him. Therefore grace is free to whosoever would repent and believe.

Grace is used as a Noun, verb or even an adjective. Knowing how it is used within the context will sometimes help to understand its meaning in the passage.

Grace is a reward to believers. At Exodus 39 Moses asked the Lord, "If I have found favor in your sight..."

Grace is Kindness:

"But Noah found grace in the eyes of The Lord (Genesis 6:8 KJV).

Grace can also be classified as the blessings promised and bestowed richly upon a believer. It is kindness, sometimes referred to as favor in regards to obedient believers. It pertains to obedience and it is conditional. In Exodus 19:5, it is talked about as belonging to the children of Israel. It can now be translated as to the church of Jesus Christ. Favorite generation, as one pastor calls it. We are the church!

Favor can be delayed:
For Discussion study: Exodus 33 and 34

This may raise some eyebrows to the carnal minded Christians, but it is scriptural. Study this passage in Exodus 19:5, 6 for discussion. I love the thought of being a favorite generation. It was by choice to accept the finished work on the cross and place absolutely all confidence in that event. I chose to believe the Bible and grace was given to me in return. Thank God for I did nothing to receive it. I continue to believe and rely on the finished work on the cross. You can become one too.

Favor is a gift we don't deserve. It may also be a gift given as a reward. It is comfort, and consolation. It is a means by which, when we are in right relationship, we can quickly access his blessings when in need. It is pity, it is everything we need to live a successful life. Also everything we need to be fruitful in our daily walk and relationship with our Savior. Read this book prayerfully. Share its truths with your group, and certainly with those who are lost.

Obedience:

There is no magical formula in regards to the fulfillment of his will in your life. Obedience will allow you to enjoy all of his blessings. You will receive all of the benefits. Yet there is a definite expectancy of the lord even as your expectation is of him. We have the option to choose, desire and obey the word of the lord. We do it because we love Him. Through obedience we can live a victorious life because we have been quickened by the power of his Holy Spirit and are made alive in Him. You will learn how to be kept by the sufficiency of His refining grace.

Prayer: Heavenly Father, grant us favor with you as well as with men. May your Divine grace and wisdom be upon every reader. May every word written be according to your Word and according to the integrity of my heart. Do that which only you do best. Enlighten every heart that they too may know your Divine plan. Thank you for bringing clarity to our hearts Lord. In Jesus name I pray, Amen!

Chapter 2

TRANSFORMING GRACE

"For by grace are ye saved through faith; and that not of yourselves: it is a gift of God; least any man should boast." (Ephesians 2:8, 9)

In studying the gift of Salvation, I decided to talk to others to see if they shared the same sentiments or belief as me. I wanted to know their understanding or perception concerning the topic of: Saved, or salvation and being born again. This term is commonly used, by most people, to describe their experience. The question I posed was very simple. I asked, "What do you mean when you say I am saved?" or "What is your understanding of salvation?" I realized the answer was incorrect, many times, or just not thought out. It was a spontaneous response perhaps derived from an opinion formed in their mind or the result of a previous teaching. I'm not saying the response was right or wrong. Based on my immediate observation some of them had no clue. As believers they were entertaining a more secular or religious point of view based on what they had learned, and not necessarily through studying the Scriptures. Some attributed it to a religion or going to a particular church.

A common response was, "I know God is real, or I belong to a certain denomination or church body." In dealing with the ones who sustained a relationship with Jesus, their response was more defined, yet some somewhat shallow. It is time for the body of Christ to understand 'saving grace, love and divine favor'. Only through grace can we have complete access to the Father, and it is only through the Son. This is the Father's desire for everyone. His grace enables us and gives us the ability to cry, "Abba Father" as believers through the shed blood of Jesus. Those outside of Christ who have not yet experienced a relationship with the Son, do not have the same privileges or benefits. This differentiates the believer, from the unbeliever, although both are equally loved by the Father. God loves his creation. Grace is not based on love. It is based on repentance and believing on Jesus.

Christ opened the door giving us access to all of the riches of His glory, but it also takes grace or favor to walk out our salvation in victory. After salvation we have an assignment to fulfill. However, without this knowledge, it might be difficult to be of influence to others. We must seek God and inquire in his word concerning his plan for us. It is not enough to know: "I am saved, sanctified and filled with the Holy Spirit, and I'm going to heaven when I die." An informed believer understands the gift and grace of God and the great responsibility that accompanies the gift as well.

They learn to witness to the lost, and to those with whom they come in contact. God is depending on the Body of Believers to proclaim the good news, (affirm and declare it with authority). To tell others what things the cross and the shedding of His blood have wrought. It is of utmost importance that we understand the inheritance through the New Covenant.

What will you render in return?

Through knowledge and love for him we will be able to reciprocate the same to others, giving grace for grace. "I love him because he first loved me" the Bible says. Not only should we give time and money, but a total commitment as well. Nothing is too much to render to God in return for our salvation. Because of gratitude there may be a desire to give something back. I am reminded of the leprous king who was told by Elijah to go wash in the Jordan. After his healing he insisted on blessing the man of God in return. When David was thirsty, his men broke through enemy lines to bring him water. He felt unworthy to partake of it and poured it on the ground seeing that they had endangered their lives. In the New Testament, Zaccheus wanted to repay and restore everything he had taken unlawfully. How much more grateful should we be to Jesus for what He has done. Nothing can repay the Savior.

In the beginning God created and made everything beautiful for his pleasure and purpose. Adam and Eve would often enjoy the presence of Jehovah in the garden, until they sinned. The Bible says in Genesis 3, that God came down and walked with them in the cool part of the day. When they heard him they were afraid because they had sinned and so they hid themselves. Prior to this, sin did not exist. They lived in a time of innocence.

Because of the sin of disobedience they were driven out of the garden and from his presence. Since that time, because of sin and transgression against God, Paradise was lost including all of us in sin. Man was separated from his maker and such a beautiful union ended in a divorce. Death passed on to all men. (Romans 5:12). But Oh! The grace of God was extended to us. His redeeming power brought salvation to all who would believe in Him. The scriptures declare, "For God so loved the world; He gave his only begotten Son that whosoever believeth on him would not perish but have everlasting life." Jesus is the only begotten of God full of grace and truth. He came as a priceless gift to redeem every sinner. He sacrificed his life and died on a cruel cross for wicked men. He was crucified for our sin, and every other sin that man would commit. By way of the blood, we now have forgiveness, and access to God. God is sovereign. Because of his great love for his creation He devised a plan to redeem us back to himself. Also, because God is Holy, sin had to be justly punished. Again, thank God for the blood and the blessed cross of Calvary.

The coming of the Redeemer:

Abraham's belief in God was accounted unto him as righteousness. This led us to Moses and the law. Men continued to disobey the commandments. We know the story of the children of Israel, when delivered from Egypt, they mumbled and complained. And with a mighty outstretched hand, God brought them into the promise land. Later the judges began to rule. They continued to ask for a king to rule over them like the neighboring nations; and so they were given good and bad kings. This also failed. They continued in idolatry and disobedience. Then, God began to speak through the Prophets which they also stoned and rejected. So when the fullness of time had come God sent forth his Son Jesus. He came as a babe, and was born in a manger and was wrapped in swaddling clothes. He came to redeem mankind. "For the grace that brings salvation hath appeared unto all men." (Titus 2:11.) This was God's best to His people, even while yet in sin. God in his sovereignty, by the Power of his Holy Spirit, caused all things to be, that were not. He granted to us the fulfillment of his promise of a savior, Emmanuel, which translates as God with us (Mathew 1:23). I feel like right about now we should be rejoicing, amen!

Sin has a penalty:

"For the wages of sin is death; but the gift of God is eternal life through Jesus Christ our Lord." (Romans 6: 23).

There is a price to be paid for sin. But thanks be unto God who sent his Son Jesus to pay the price for us. Now we are privilege to live a transformed (changed, renewed) life, one that brings glory to Him. God has never rewarded sin, however he does honor obedience with peace, joy, and eternal life.

What is Sin?

According to the PC Bible (New Unger's Dictionary) SIN: in Hebrew it is chata'ah and in the

Greek it is Hamartia. It is also falling away from or missing the right path. Others refer to this Hebrew word as an archer aiming and missing the mark. A pastor friend of mine often relates to sin as: a mistake in one's identity. I concur with that concept, in that everything we do should reflect the image and character of our creator. We are made in his image. As new creatures in Christ we are called to represent Him. Therefore, any misconduct or flaw in our character denotes a contradiction in whom and whose we are. It also signifies if there has been any change or transformation in our growth and maturity subsequent to our conversion. According to the Scripture at 2 Corinthians 5:17, "Therefore if any man be in Christ, (he or she) is a new creature; old things are passed away; behold, all things are become new." Though the old man is dead we can certainly resurrect him, and walk according to our flesh. Why? Because we turned away and lost track of our image in the law of liberty, which is the Word of God. Staying in the Word will cleanse us, and keep us on the narrow path if we seek to do so from the heart.

It is written in the Unger's Bible saying: "In general the underlying idea of sin is that of law and of a lawgiver. The lawgiver is God. Therefore, sin is everything in the disposition, purpose and conduct of God's moral creatures contrary to his expressed will.

(Romans 3: 17; 4: 15; 7: 7; James 4: 12, 17). It is also stated that: "The sinfulness of sin lies in the fact that it is against God. Even when the wrong we do, is to others or ourselves." See (Gen 39:9; Ps 51:4). It is also said that when sin is put in the place of God, in nature, it is egotism and selfishness.

Scriptures to study: The law has a purpose. No one is more righteous than the other under the law, Jews and gentiles alike. The law makes us conscious of sin. (Romans 3:20; 4:15; 7:7; James 4:12, 17).

Sin is an offense, and it is contrary to his law through disobedience. It alters and changes the plans of God for all mankind, bringing us all under the curse of the law. Romans 5:12, states: "Wherefore, as by one man's sin entered into the world and death by sin; and so death passed upon all men, for that all have sinned. Verse-17, "For if by one man's offence death reigned by one; much more they which receive abundance of grace and of the gift of righteousness shall reign in life by one, Jesus Christ." Here we see the principle of the power of one. We may recall an incident throughout our own life whereby the opinion or approval of one individual was vital for a final decision in a matter relating to us.

Question: In your words: What is salvation?

Answer: Delivered from anything that impedes or prevents you from attaining Gods highest or what He has intended for your life. (see other definitions below)

Soterion: (So-tay'-ree-on): Rescue, deliver, protect, save, healing, health, whole, defender.

"By grace are ye saved and not of yourselves it is a gift of God lest any man should boast."

Gift: Something acquired without compensation, a present, needs no repayment. Jesus is the greatest gift to us. It is written that God so loved the world He gave his only begotten Son that through Him we might be saved and again come into a right relationship with him.

As a rule, a gift is a present. Sometimes gifts are not appreciated. Jesus gave us the gift of grace whereby we are saved. It is the gift of God. Meaning, God gave us freely the ability to know Him and the Son whom He sent; this is eternal life, as declared by the scriptures. Some years ago I worked at a large nursing home. One day a patient of mine contacted the administration of that facility in order to give me a gift. She was not confused. And though she went through the proper channel, it was denied. According to them it was due to hospital policy. It was a burgundy swayback Victorian chair, in mint condition. I couldn't help from entertaining the thought of the wonderful gift, how beautiful it would look in my bedroom. We were both disappointed. The next day she called me in the room. She could not understand why she couldn't give away something that belonged to her. She stated it belonged to her deceased mother, and she wanted me to have it. After a while she placed something into my pocket, and said: "That chair may have been too large to carry out of the door, but this is not. She then proceeded to push me through the door before I could say anything else. Later I checked my pocket and discovered she had tucked a beautiful emerald ring in it. She told me it was a gift from her deceased mother given to her many years prior. She insisted that I take it. This was something she had cherished for years.

Can you imagine the gift He gives us? It cannot be taken away or denied. All we have to do is receive it by faith. Jesus paid the price in advance with His blood. It was the ultimate sacrifice of the Father, given to us, His only Son. Therefore, there is no compensation necessary. Man did not deserve it, and it cannot be earned. It is only through the unmerited favor of God. "For by grace are ye saved through faith; and that not of yourselves: It is a gift of God: not of works lest any man should boast." Thank God no human intervention was needed in order for us to partake of this gift. I remember on one occasion thinking about something I could wear that was cool enough for the mission trip to Panama. I needed something that was not too warm for the weather. Suddenly, the telephone rang. On the other end was my friend Earline Stack. She said, "Hey Gina, my daughter just emptied her closet and I thought about you." I told her I would be home for the evening and she could stop by anytime. The next week I had to minister. Again, I needed something I could wear afterwards to the church picnic. This was only a thought in my mind. How amazing that God would hear my faintest thought. Saturday evening there was another call by my friend. She said, "Hey! I have this dress with the tags still on it, I though you could wear it. I will bring it right over if you are going to be there." With my hands raised and with gratitude and amazement I said, "God. . . you did it again!"

A few days later, I was sitting at the breakfast table thinking about how good God was to me. I also thought of how she (Earlene) had blessed me, and I had nothing to give to her in return. Quietly I thought, perhaps I should get her a gift of some sort. Then suddenly I was reminded of a previous lesson I had studied on the subject: "What is a gift?" Immediately, I understood why people sometimes find it difficult to receive a gift from others. I realized how they felt. Some perhaps may feel unworthy. Others may have a sense of guilt. I Repented before God and prayed a prayer saying, "Lord forgive me for not putting into practice what you have taught me."

What is grace? Grace is something we have freely obtained, and as believers we also should give to others. God gave us grace instead of punishment or judgment we rightly deserved. Yet, sometimes we may all find it difficult to show the same to others. Especially if we have been offended by them. Though it cost us nothing, yet, it cost Christ everything. We ought to give grace for grace; after all it was free to us.

Grace: is a force or power. To try to describe it is like trying to describe God. Graciousness, figuratively or spiritually. It is especially the divine influence upon the heart of men. It is a cognitive factor that has an effect on what we do or how we respond.

Grace is what God is free to do and indeed does it according to His Sovereign Will. It is merited only through repentance and accepting Christ who died for us by faith. Thank you Lord, for you have chosen to bless me with divine favor. The songwriter puts it this way: "Your grace and mercy brought me through and I am living this moment because of you".

The grace of God is undeniable, indescribably amazing! It surpasses our understanding. (Titus 3:5a NIV) says: "He saved us, not because of righteous things we had done, but because of his mercy." Grace is giving us what we did not deserve while mercy is withholding from us what we rightly deserved, (punishment, and death alienation).

Again, I like what Paul said in Ephesians, "O the depth of the riches, both of the wisdom and knowledge of God! How unsearchable are his judgments, and his ways past finding out!" We will never get to the end of grace, even as we cannot get to the end of God. Because it is so vastly defined. According to the NIV (New International Version) grace is mentioned (8) times in the Old Testament and 133 times in the New Testament. In the KJV (King James Version) it is said to be found (39) times in the Old Testament, and (131) times, in the New Testament. Imagine this, even without considering other translations. It is already too much to explore other versions.

However, the important thing is for us to have some kind of understanding. We must also get a clear revelation of what Grace is, more than only the unmerited favor of God. But know also that it is these as well: Our help, kindness, thankfulness, power, beauty and much more extended to us. All of which relates to the character or attributes of Christ in our lives. Further in the lesson we will attempt to deal with the word Grace in a more in-depth way, outlining only a few scriptures. As we seek more truth to this Word, know that without faith it will not be fully appreciated. (I will not deal with faith in its context at this time). Although grace does not work without it. They go hand in hand. Even as His love. God is love. Grace is accessed by faith; it can also be increased and multiplied according to the scriptures.

Grace: benefit, gift, favor

Chen (khane: favor, graciousness, kindness, pleasant, precious, and well-favored. Objectively it means beauty (New Unger's dictionary).

1. *Question*: What is the consequence of sin?

Answer: According to (Romans 6:23) "For the wages of sin is death." But God's gift to us is eternal life.

2. *Question*: Will God take His gifts away from us?
Answer: "For the gifts and calling of God are without repentance." (Romans 11:29)

3. *Question*: Do we have to recompense the gift?
Answer: Not by works lest any man should boast." (Ephesians 3:9)

4. *Question*: What was God's gift to the human race?

Answer: When the time was fully come, God sent his

Son" (Galatians 4:4)

Summarize and discuss the principles of Grace.

Thank God for His grace which brought salvation? It delivers, justifies, and redeems us from the curse of sin. It's Amazing. The Bible declares: "For the grace of God that brings salvation hath appeared to all men." (Titus 2:11.) Grace came to fight for us; it transforms, as well as heals us. Without God we are nothing, neither can we do anything without His grace. While traveling to other parts of the world, observing their culture, I get to see both sides of the spectrum. How they hunger and thirst for the things we take so lightly. Can you imagine what the Father feels when he looks at the situation? I believe he sees the lack of concern for heavenly things, and for fellowshipping with Him. He gave his best, and how selfish we can be at times. On the mission field I get to see the poor for whom Jesus died living below the poverty level. While others enjoy the luxury of this world. I see a people though different in culture and language, believing God for salvation for their families, themselves, for their government, and their nation as well. I also often see leaders coming together to pray and fellowship; bowing to the ground under the open heavens crying out with humility to Jehovah saying, "Spare your people Oh Lord!" As they seek after Him. Yes, seeking. Like the woman with the issue of blood, bound for 12 years, who followed

Jesus. Thinking in her mind, "If I could—but touch him." "O If only I could-touch the hem—of his garment, I know I will be healed."

Remember the Syrophenecian woman, who sought Jesus for deliverance for her demoniac daughter? Who also changed the course of history (the law) that day. Though she was ignored she was relentless in her plea, and refused to be denied. She reminded him that even the dogs ate the crumbs that fell from their masters table. It was no fault of `hers that her daughter had a demon. Likewise today we may encounter others who are victims with or without any fault of their own. As believers our duty is to pray and intercede for them. We must bear one another's burden, praying one for another.

Consider the case of these two sisters Mary and Martha seeking Jesus for their brother Lazarus, looking to the resurrection. But Jesus had the power to raise him from the dead that day. The blood of bulls or goats could not do it. It was only a shadow of that which was to come. "And almost all things are by the law purged with at the patterns of things in heavens should be purified with these; but the heavenly things themselves with better sacrifices than these. For Christ is not entered into the Holy place made with hands, which are the figures of the true;

but into heaven itself, now to appear in the presence of God for us". (Hebrews 9:22-24) (Great passage for discussion).

I am moved by this passage each time I read it. It causes me to offer up a sacrifice of praise. Having knowledge of the reality that Jesus paid such an awesome price, not to be compared to that of animals. The pattern demonstrated purification by the blood was not only necessary, but also, a requirement, according to the law. Wherefore, we know that Christ paid an awesome sacrifice. When he offered up his life it provided a better covenant, making it possible for all mankind to appear before the Father, once again and in the ages that were to come.

Scriptural passages on grace for discussion:

• "Therefore, as ye abound in everything in faith and utterance, and knowledge, and in all diligence, and in your love to us, see that ye abound in this grace also." (2 Corinthian 8:7)

• "By whom also we have access by faith into this grace wherein we stand and rejoice in hope of the glory of God." (Romans 5:2)

• "And not that only, but who was also chosen of the churches to travel with us with this grace, which is administered by us to the glory of the same Lord, and declaration of your ready mind." (2 Corinthians 8:19)

More on grace:

It was in 1998, when I first started looking at the subject of grace. I was then prompted by the Holy Spirit to take a deeper look at it. I became leery and hesitant to share this revelation with anyone. My eyes were open to a great truth. Because it was new to me. I was afraid it would be rejected. I did not feel I had enough scriptural knowledge to base my findings, and I did not want to be misunderstood by those who perhaps didn't share the same opinion on the subject. And who might think I was introducing some new doctrine. I had not heard it preached before at that time, except as the unmerited favor, which it is. However, I knew there was more to grace than the familiar saying: "He didn't have to do it, but He did". I refer to this as "sloppy grace". Especially when it is used to excuse and justify sin. In other words: One can live any kind of way, do whatever he or she pleases (without repentance). Continue practicing sin, yet use grace to justify themselves.

I knew God delighted in holiness and obedience. I also knew he desired more from me, and he wanted to do a greater work in my life. Therefore I would have to please him in all of my ways, and he would show me his divine favor. I remember speaking to Sister Naomi, my pastor's wife in Arkansas, I shared with her what I believed the Lord had shown me at that time. I remember telling her, "I don't know, but I believe grace is more than the unmerited favor of God. It's more that is said to be in lay terms. "He didn't have to do it, but he did." Grace can be tapped into. It can also be accelerated and multiplied by believers who understand their inheritance as heirs of his promise through the blood.

"Grace and peace be multiplied unto you through the knowledge of God, and of Jesus our Lord. According as his divine power hath given unto us all things that pertained unto life and godliness, through the knowledge of him that hath called us to glory and virtue." (2 Peter 1:2, 3) It is power given unto us. It comes more so through obedience and faith in his word. Therefore being justified by faith, we have peace with God through our Lord Jesus Christ: By whom also we have access by faith into this grace wherein we stand, and rejoice in hope of the glory of God.

It wasn't long after this that I visited a friend in Phoenix Arizona. We attended a Wednesday night service. Some would say this was a coincidence, I say it was divine providence. During the service the pastor, Keith A. Butler, taught on Grace. When I heard it, I almost fell off my chair from the excitement. I had a time! On the inside I was shouting: "I knew it, I knew there was something to it."

At the end of the service he gave away a few copies of his latest book. Guess what! I was the first one he chose to receive one. This was a divine appointment with destiny for me that day. To top it off, the title of the book was none other than, "The Grace of God." Because of the delicateness of the subject of grace, I chose not to focus on too many areas except on those which have been revealed to me. I strongly recommend that you read the book entitled: "The Grace of God", by Keith A. Butler for further enlightenment or for a more in-depth study on the subject of Grace.

Other supporting scriptures for study:

(**2 Corinthians 12:9**) "He said unto me, my grace is sufficient for thee."

(**James 4:6**) "But, He giveth more grace, wherefore he saith God resisting the proud but giveth grace to the humble."

(**2 Peter 1:2**) "Grace and peace be multiplied unto you through the knowledge of God, and of Jesus our Lord."

Prayer: Father, I thank you and bless you for sending me your grace. May you open our hearts and eyes. Enlighten us to the truth of your word, that we may be better prepared in our service to you. I pray also Heavenly Father you give us minds that are ready to partake of your blessings through faith. In the name of Jesus, Amen . . . . !

Chapter 3

The Cross: The Object of Faith

"Looking unto Jesus the author and finisher of our faith; who for the joy that was set before him, endured the cross, despising the shame, and is set down at the right hand of the throne of God." (Hebrews 12:2).

The cross is the only thing that matters. It is our only hope of salvation through the blood of Jesus. Meaning if we get Jesus wrong, the entire equation is wrong. The cross entails life as well as death. Have you ever stopped to wonder, "Where would we be without the cross?" It is the duty and personal responsibility of every believer to understand God's redemption plan for mankind. Therefore, every believer should be able to render an explanation concerning the hope that lies within him or her, which is Christ in him or her, the hope of glory. Then go and proclaim the Good News with those who are lost. Take in view, this does not mean you have to be of the clergy or five-fold ministry such as: Apostle, Prophet, Evangelist, Pastor and teacher.

Let's look at some Scriptures dealing with the

cross and the grace of God. It is such a vast subject, the Holy Spirit has to make it known to our spirit. He reveals to us that which He wants us to know.

The Scripture declares: "The Spirit himself will bear witness to our spirit." Bear in mind, each time we behold Him in worship or read the word we can be assured we are looking directly in the face of the resurrected Christ, God almighty. He is God with us, Emmanuel. The one who died and rose again, and is soon to return for his bride, the church. This is that same Jesus who walked on the shores of Galilee.

Follow after Jesus:

Scriptures for discussion. Matthew 6:24, Mark 8:34, Luke 9:23 says, "...if any man will come after me, let him deny himself, pick up his cross daily, and follow me." Notice it is an invitation to all, but there is a requirement to take up your cross. The decision is yours, to follow. You allow yourself, and you deny yourself. It does not say He will do this for you. You decide how close you want to follow. However, He is looking for those who will follow closely in His footstep.

The purpose of the church is to go and make disciples through the preaching of the cross. The gospel is the only thing that changes the heart of men.

It is not about us, but about the people of the world that do not know Christ. He prepares us to go and meet the needs, be a solution to the problem. We are not to become part of the problem.

I believe we miss the mark whenever we try to change circumstances in people, instead of changing their hearts through the gospel. And yes we are called to go and make followers, disciples for Jesus. This is the quest of the great commission of which we are called. It may entail meeting their needs when necessary in order to reach them, prepare them that they in turn may also go and do likewise. However, this is not suggesting we don't feed the hungry or heal the sick or do any of the other things that accompanies the gospel. It is not to be the primary assignment. We do it by doing these other things, the goal is that men may be saved.

The Lord is the Shepherd and provider. He meets the need through us.

I see a great need for evangelism amongst believers, especially for personal evangelism. In many cases, teaching is vital for believers to know their purpose which is for them to go and make other disciples.

Many times whenever I minister abroad, I will

ask the congregation: "How many of you are preparing to go?" There is seldom any answer or a show of hands, especially in the women. I'm not saying they aren't. In proportion to the universal call and expectation Jesus exclaimed, "The fields are white for harvest, but where are the laborers?" We even see it in the book of Joel. "Where are the sons and daughters who are to prophesy in these last dark and evil days?" I am hopeful it will come. I am reminded of a story I heard entitled "Great stories of the Bible" from the Moodie broadcast. It was said of Mr. Francis Asbury, a pioneer from England during the 18th century. According to Mr. Francis Asbury, "There is a great work going on in America, but there is still much more to be done." Later that year on October 7th he arrived in Philadelphia. I'm amazed at what he said then. I believe in some circumstances the same can be said today, "There is still a great work to be done." We must get ready for the Lord's return. God wants to show his glory through every believer. His words are sure and he will honor it, He has never failed.

Once as I sought the Lord for a need concerning the ministry, a minister friend of mine brought this thought back to my remembrance, which was so profound it has become the motto for the Panama Mission. She spoke these words to me saying, "Whatsoever is born of God overcomes the world."

This was fifteen years ago at the inception of the ministry of the Panama Mission Campaign, an outreach of Restorative Hope. Over the past years because of the transformation in my mind, I have seen God respond in amazing ways. I know with assurance I could not have done it without him. I have been blessed in so many ways I can't begin to tell.

The Cross:

The cross is an emblem representing suffering. People entertain different ideologies in regards to it. It talks to us of:

• Denying ourselves daily.

• It teaches us the importance of commitment.

• It requires true dedication.

In today's world it is difficult to find people who truly manifest these three principles demonstrated by the Lord Jesus, who was faithful. He did it without reservation.

The most important thing is, the cross speaks about what Jesus did for us all with his own body on the tree. It is about Golgotha in the Hebrew, interpreted in Latin as Calvary. I often stop to think of that old familiar song, "On a hill far away, The Old

Rugged Cross". Then came the day I actually stood in front of it in Jerusalem. This song has become an anthem to me on the mission field watching the tears, the brokeness on the faces of even the little children as they in unison, synphonically sings the words.

Seek to understand Him:

It is important for us in these perilous times that we seek to know God for ourselves. I believe if one earnestly pray and seek after Him more than just in a casual way, a better understanding is inevitable.

The importance of the Cross:

The cross is the object of our faith. We are admonished that in all of our getting we should get understanding. And above all we need to get wisdom. By studying the Word we will know and understand God's character and nature. The cross is the beginning place of your encounter with the Lord. It is a place of intimacy and of a new love relationship with the Father, who is our creator. It is also the dividing line between life and death. Saved or lost. Blessed or cursed. It is a place of repentance, where we make the choice between the broad road that leads to destruction, or the narrow path that leads to life eternal.

One songwriter pens it like this, "At the cross at the

cross where I first saw the light and the burdens of my heart rolled away. It was there by faith I received my sight and now I am happy all the day."

Sight is Light:

Spiritual sight comes through receiving the Christ of that cross. We also have physical sight. Is light truly sweet for me at this time?

Each time I read this Scripture it causes me to look into the face of God as a child looks into his daddy's face. It's almost as though saying, "Lord, don't forget me!" the preacher in Ecclesiastes 11:7, proclaimed a truth that often touches my spirit. Though it seems contrary, I dare not refute God. It says, "Truly light is sweet, and a pleasant thing it is for the eyes to behold the sun." Every time I'm bothered by the sun I quote it with expectancy, proclaiming to God his own word. Why is it not pleasant to me, Lord? The reason it is so beautiful is because Jesus is the light of the sun. Imagine for a moment the yearning we sense especially after a long winter, or in the night season. How we long to see a sunny day. I've yet to see someone who is always as enthusiastic about the dark as they are about the sunshine. There is something about the sunlight that refreshes our soul, and causes complete altering in our perspective of life. Suddenly life seems to have more meaning.

It gives a feeling of being rejuvenated. You will find everyone commenting about how beautiful the day is. Notice the contrast on a bleak or dreary day. The comments are no longer positive and cheerful, but almost as though complaining. I can attest to this because whenever I'm exposed to direct light, natural or artificial, I am often bothered by the blinding effects of the glare, even the least amount. Although it is blinding, yet I desperately need the light in order to see or perform any kind of task. It's an in betwixt and in between situation for me. Nevertheless, I thank God for the sun. It does my spirit good each time I see the light of day. I'm looking forward to that day when my healing manifests itself. Therefore, I will say with a jubilant shout, "I once was blind, but now I can see!"

Some may have found the cross to be a place of comfort when in trouble. (We may also relate this equally to the church, as a similar example in some regards). Spiritually speaking, it is a place we can run to. While lots of people have attested to this, some hang around finding no comfort. "Don't linger around without knowing whom you are seeking." Some perhaps have found it to be a good place to be with others or to go on special occasions, perhaps because of traditional upbringing, yet doing nothing of consequence to enhance the Kingdom. In the book of Hebrews chapter 6, the Apostle Paul says: "Therefore leaving the principles of the doctrine of Christ, let us go on unto perfection; not laying again the foundation of repentance from dead works, and of faith toward God, Of the doctrine of baptism, and of the laying on of hands, and of resurrection of the dead, and of eternal judgment." This is a command and not an option.

It is something God expects of every believer. A delayed response on our part is like blatant disobedience. By no means is this saying to put away our salvation, neither is it referring to it as something insignificant. Salvation is the most important step an individual can make in his or her life. It is a step toward God and advancement toward the Kingdom. What He is saying is, don't remain there. Move on to maturity and to the weightier matters of your salvation, so that you might be used by Him, and receive the promises. Grow in grace and in the purpose of the Father. Go on to baptism. Go on to the laying on of hands. Be empowered and receive the gift of the Holy Spirit for the greater works as it is written in the Scriptures. Wherefore, it is the duty of every man, woman, boy and girl to become a witness for Christ. Don't be satisfied with merely being saved and sanctified. Become a blessing to others and profitable for the kingdom, to usher in the return of our blessed Savior.

I believe it is an outright shame for us to receive salvation, to sit on the pews for years never doing anything to advance the Kingdom, or for the furtherance of the gospel, sitting around awaiting a reward in Heaven when we die.

Discussion- Hebrews chapter 6:

• Question: How does this passage speak to you?

• Question: What advancement have you made since your salvation?

• Question: How have you contributed to the Kingdom since your salvation?

"It was through what his Son did that God cleared a pathway; so that everyone could come to Him through Christ.

Christ's death on the cross has made peace for all through the blood. (Colossians 1:20)

"To every thing there is a season..." (Ecclesiastes 3:1)

After salvation we must steadily advance into the deeper things of God. Those things which are not natural, but also spiritual in nature.

There must be a time whereby you begin to eat

solid food, instead of milk. Sometimes the lack of involvement may well be one of the reasons some saints, perhaps, become so needy, never having any time to be of help to others, always needing help themselves. Again, I say; "Never lose sight of the cross, neither your purpose", it is the main object of your faith.

Just as we have natural changes in the seasons; (Summer, Winter, Spring, and Fall), so are the seasonal changes that accompany our salvation. They are changes that take place in the seasons of life. In some instances as we mature, the process may be painful. The Scriptures declare in Psalms 71, read it and be blessed how David petitioned God. Even in old age we can yet be profitable to God. In other words, we may experience what others deem as growth pains. But greater yet we will also experience moments of joy. We should rejoice in both, joy and in tribulation as well. After experiencing the cross it is imperative that we unite with other believers in order to get the full benefits, and continue to grow as newborn babes in Christ. The next step is to find a place of worship, as intended by God. As we unite we will receive, (Fellowship, Friendship and Followship). A three-fold blessing, which are all benefits of the cross. Just remember, "Do not remain in your comfort zone" lest you run the risk of your faith becoming stagnated, because faith cometh by hearing and hearing by the Word. You must be in the right place or position to hear when He softly whispers your name and invites you to follow saying; "Come follow me." It is important we respond immediately leaving all, as the disciples did and according to the gospel.

In order to live it is important we die:

No one likes to hear about death, however in order for us to live, we must first be ready to die. We will not grow unless we die to self (flesh), and to sin.

Our flesh is constantly at war with the Spirit, as well as the spirit to the flesh. Death to the flesh only comes by way of the cross. Contrary to other beliefs. Jesus Christ is the only way. He died that men may live and have the right to eternal life. In 1Corinthians 15:22 Paul spoke these words, "For as in Adam all die, even so in Christ shall all be made alive." He recognized what it meant to die when he said, "For me to live is Christ and to die is gain."

It was necessary for Christ to die and be resurrected. What he couldn't do in that he was in the flesh, identifying himself with humanity; he did this by offering himself once and for all on a cruel cross called Calvary. To pay the price to satisfy the wrath of the Father. Willingly He offered up himself. The shedding of his blood remitted sin so that there was no longer a need for an offering, he became the ultimate sacrifice, a picture of GRACE.

The promise of The Holy Spirit:

The seal to our salvation through the Holy Spirit. Henceforth, he did not leave us comfortless, but sent us his Holy Spirit as was promised and written by the prophets of old. Which promise came on the day of Pentecost? The comforter the Holy Spirit is here to lead and guide us into all truth. He walks in us as well as beside us daily; talking to us, and revealing unto us the will of the Father. "Howbeit when he, the Spirit of truth, is come, he will guide you into all truth." (John 16:13)

What is the Cross?

According to the talking dictionary: "The cross is a pole with a transverse post. It is widely recognized as an emblem of Christianity. It also refers to any kind of affliction that causes suffering. The Scriptures declare, we all have a cross to bear. It also states that if we look back, we are not worthy to follow Him. There is a very familiar passage in the Old Testament in Isaiah 53, which vividly depicts a picture of Christ's suffering. He suffered and hung on a cruel cross despising the shame, because of his great love for the world.

Self Denial:

"Placing urgency on the mind. Demanding insistence and consistency. It is to put pressure on the mind." It prohibits the flesh from ruling.

It is also considered as an archer shooting an arrow, trying to hit the bulls-eye.

Stauros (stow-ros'): "A stake or post set upright. Specifically a pole or cross, as an instrument of capital punishment. A tree. Figuratively, exposure to death, i.e. self-denial, by implication, (the atonement of Christ. In searching the scriptures it was difficult to pin point one particular area dealing with the cross without the involvement of other subjects such as: self-denial, mercy, love kindness etc).

It seems to me as though, the preaching of the cross has been forgotten or greatly diminished in some churches. Instead of Good News it has become as old news, as journalism instead of evangelism. Sometimes the attitude appears to be that of, "I have heard that sermon before. Let us hear something more interesting and exciting." It has perhaps become that as of a spirit of slumber or indifference; it may well have over-shadowed some churches.

Nevertheless, those who experience a true relationship, who are hungry, usually obtained a genuine revelation. Their experience remains fresh. People who believe are always blessed. The Bible says if we seek we will find and will be filled. But it's to those who seek, this is what makes the difference with believers.

I have always treasured the old songs about the cross and I'm often broken by some of the lyrics. These are the songs which brought me to Jesus. Hymns that pricked my soul. I was touched by them time and time again and understood the realness of the cross. I'm saddened each time I hear loose comments concerning some of the old gospel hymns. To some they may seem as taboo and out dated. Yet, I enjoy most songs even some of the gospel Rapp. I have trained my mind to listen to the words. If I can't seem to get with the song I tell my flesh, "After all Gina, they are not singing to you anyway, but to God." This usually brings me back into check, (a mental alignment). When we understand what the cross has wrought for us and its total significance, we will become more sensitive and more apt to worship the one who, though he was faultless, hung there willingly.

The apostle Paul declared, "I press towards the prize for the mark of the high calling in Christ Jesus." (Philippians 3:14 KJV.)

Here is an acronym for the word (Push), it is to:

P—persist U—until S—something H—happens

Press or push towards the mark or expectant goal. It also means to persevere, or be insistent. Make a demand on with force. In essence Paul is saying, "We can place urgency on our mind." Make a demand on your faith with insistence. It is as though putting pressure on your desire. It is being unshakable, grounded and unmovable. To be established. The mark is considered as that of an archer shooting an arrow, aiming, to hit a bulls-eye.

Every believer should have a clear view of the way things are in their life. As some would say, "Get your ducks in a row." Be honest with yourself. Where are you in the press? We cheat ourselves out of a blessing or an increase in knowledge when we deny, or deceive ourselves in thinking all is well. It may be a good practice to make frequent examination of your own self. See whether you are still in the race or in faith. Know that if there is any lack, God will make up the difference whenever you are intentional in doing so. The Scriptures put it this way, "And if at some point you think differently, that too God will make clear to you. Only let us live up to what we already attained. Join with others, following by example; brothers take note of those who live according to the pattern we gave you. For as I have often told you before now say again even with tears, Many live as enemies of the cross of Christ." (Philippians 3:15-18 NKJV.) A word of caution, we could be in jeopardy with God, by merely thinking differently than what we have obtained, or been taught. We must take heed to the Word, least we come short of obtaining every promise He has for us. The Scriptures also reveal to us how we should live, pressing towards the mark of the high call in Christ Jesus. Having this mindset comes with maturity in the Word and to have any other mindset or aim, we become as enemies of the cross.

Reckon yourself dead to self, and to the works of the flesh:

Reckon: • Have faith or confidence in. • Consider or deem to be. • Make a mathematical calculation or computation in your mind.

The key is to reckon ourselves delivered from sin. Having a daily confession, studying, and getting the Word in us, will help ground and establish us in the truth. This is something you do through faith, based on what God has already done and said in his

Word. This is based on your conviction and knowledge of the truth, what you choose to rely on, God's Word or what others say about it. It's imperative we believe the Word regardless of feelings or our human understanding.

If we have been forgiven of our transgressions against the Father, and washed in the blood of Jesus, we are no longer bound to the law of sin. However, it is our responsibility to walk in the knowledge of this truth. Gain knowledge of what it means to reckon ourselves-dead to sin, according to the Word. We have been given the power to abstain from every sin even the appearance of it. Paul says that we are free because the law of the Spirit of life in Christ has already freed and rendered us not guilty, justified in the eyes of the Father. Henceforth, we are no longer under condemnation. "There is therefore now no condemnation to them which are in Christ Jesus, who walk not after the flesh, but after the Spirit." (Romans 8:1).

It is not automatic just because you have received Christ as your savior. Without your acknowledgement and quest to obey, the stipulation is clear. If after salvation we continue to walk after the flesh in an unrepentant state, sin will continue to reign. We run the risk of suffering condemnation.

Thank God for the advocate we have with the Father in Christ. If we confess our faults and sins, He is faithful and just (without making any qualms) to forgive us and cleanse us from all unrighteousness. This is one of many key points which must not be overlooked or taken lightly in regards to the grace of God. The apostle Paul made another profound statement when he said, "I am crucified with Christ never the less I live; yet not I, but Christ liveth in me: and the life which I now live in the flesh I live by the faith of the Son of God, who loved me, and gave himself for me (Galatians 2:20 KJV).

I believe as believers we too can live a surrendered life dying daily to the evil dictates of our hearts. Yes, there will be struggles, and yes we may even faint sometimes. But thanks be unto God who giveth us the victory always and causes us to triumph in all places. Whatever you struggle with may well be the thing to enslave you and hold you captive. I perceive that Paul endeavored to make a point when he said in that particular passage, "...that he was dead to sin, to the law and to the world as well." I believe He meant just what He said. It is evident when you examine His life. He became insensitive to every appeal of the flesh. According to, (Barnes note) He also said, sin had no more dominion over him. It no longer reigned in his mortal body. We can make this choice as believers in Christ also.

What is the law?

According to the PC Bible KJV: Nomos, (nom'-os). Refers to regulation, specifically of Moses. Including the volume; also of the Gospel. Figuratively a principle. I like the definition that is given here: (figuratively a principle.) I realize, we live by the principles of the Scriptures. They help us to have a better understanding of what the Word is saying to us. By putting the knowledge we obtain into practice, integrating it into our daily lives, it is considered as using wisdom. Wisdom is also defined as the act of our obedience. Knowledge bringing us into a more intimate relationship with the Lord, who would rather for us to obey than to offer up sacrifice or penance afterwards.

Repentance says, "I have changed my mind. I will not commit this lewd act against you any longer Lord." While penance says, "I will attend church every day Lord. I will give all of my money in the offering. Or, I won't lie for a week. Lord, you know I'm weak, but you are still working on me." Of course we know all of this is unacceptable behavior in the sight of the Lord. God delights in our obedience and He takes pleasure when we do what is right. All things that pertain to life and godliness has been deposited in us.

We lack no good thing because of the indwelling of His Holy Spirit. The same Spirit that raised Christ from the dead has quickened and made our mortal bodies alive, is the same Spirit that now dwells within us.

It is an awesome thought to perceive. As His children in the gospel, we have been chosen to be carriers of His glory. We possess the treasure of God in these earthen vessels of clay. We have been sanctified and fit for the master's use, literally a sanctuary unto Him. This is so beautiful when we think of all that has been invested and entrusted to us. The Word in our flesh. Christ himself the hope of glory, dwelling inside of us. Perhaps we may have never given thought of the word in John chapter one which says, "The Word became flesh and dwelt amongst us." After resurrection, the same word now lives inside of us. We are the now the expression of God on the earth. God working through us by way of the gospel to bring salvation to the world He loved so much, He sent His Son to die for those who would believe.

Realizing all the qualities we possess should cause us to affirm our faith more often. When we are deliberate and intentional, that is when we are better able to execute the plan.

Therefore, when we worship the God of our

salvation it will be in spirit and in truth knowing we are fulfilling His will. Again, I have to say Wow! It is simply amazing; "How can I after knowing this, not have a change of heart?

This again is a good place to stop and give a hearty Amen! "Come on, help me lift up Jesus." Right about now let's put a Selah (pause), and praise Him. Allow me to sing a little of this familiar chorus in awe of Him, "When I think of the goodness of Jesus. And all that he's done for me." My little sanctified soul cries out Halleluiah! I thank God for saving me. You may not understand why I stop to reflect and give the Lord a praise offering. I realize had it not been for his grace, I too would be seated on the corner, or sidewalk gazing aimlessly at the sky, dirty and unkept as others I have seen. But O for the grace of God, there I go!

Today while getting dressed and putting on my blouse, I tried very hard to see myself in the mirror. Needless to say, I was not successful in finding my image anywhere. Every mirror in the house rejected me, it was as though I was not present. Finally giving up I realized what was happening. In silence I whispered a delightful prayer saying, "Daddy, I trust you. You have been so good to me, and I thank you." It's the little blessings that makes the difference, until

I can believe for bigger ones. Each day I experience God in a new way. It's a moment-by-moment journey."

Law of the Spirit of life in Christ:

There are natural laws as well as Spiritual laws. The Bible teaches us about the law of the Spirit. The ministration, function and diversity of the Spirit. its relationship to the gospel and our involvement as believers and heirs of the promise. The apostle Paul declared concerning the laws of Moses, "Will not the ministry of the Spirit be even more glorious?

(2 Corinthian 3:8). We can now expect a greater glory from the life giving Spirit than that of the ministry of death written on tablets. It is far more superb, and not at all veiled.

The Law of sin and death:

Discuss Romans 8

Sin separates us from God. It may prevent us from inheriting eternal life if we continue in it.

Scriptures for Discussion:

Revelation chapters 2, 3

Revelation 2:26 KJV, and he who overcomes, and

keeps my commandments

Revelation 3:21;

Mathew 24:13 He who overcomes will be saved.

There is a penalty to those who practice sin. "For the wages of sin is death, but the gift of God is eternal life through Christ." Romans 6:23 KJV.

You may not have considered the power of this promise. I have been guilty of sometimes reading the Bible without meditating on its sayings to me. Think about the power we have through the Holy Spirit in us, how because to that power, we are able to live a holy and righteous life if we choose to.

Sin brings reproach and disgrace or criticism to many people and to the gospel. Sin keeps us living at odds with the Lord. "For the scripture tells us, "Righteousness exalts a nation, but sin is a reproach to any people." (Proverbs 14:34)

Prayer: Holy Spirit open our eyes that through the cross of Calvary, every man, woman, boy and girl may experience your wondrous love and mercy as they continue to rely on you and walk in the truth of your word and have victory. In the matchless name of your Son Jesus Christ, Amen.

Chapter 4

Fight The Good Fight of Faith

"Fight the good fight of faith (1 Timothy 6:12)

It never seizes to amaze me when believers make comments such as, "We don't have to fight since the Holy Spirit is doing it for us," saying the battle is not ours but the Lord's. I do agree, but if you have no struggles, meaning the devil doesn't bother you, I would be inclined to question your relationship. We are told the thief is seeking to kill and destroy. I agree, though we live in the flesh we do not war in the flesh. Our weapons for warfare are not carnal weapons. We fight with truth, consistency, perseverance, love, watchfulness, total reliance, honesty, silence; we have so many spiritual weapons we don't have to put our hands in physically. The Devil is not flesh and blood, he is a spirit. It is foolish to think we can match him. Thank God Christ teaches our hands to fight that even a steel bow will be broken by our arms.

Have you thought about what the apostle Paul meant when he admonished us to fight? We have been told the battle is not ours, it is the Lord's, and that is true. The Scripture says to fight this fight of faith. And to endure hardship as a good soldier. Think about the activity of a soldier and compare it to your mindset. When a soldier enlists in the military with the understanding he may not survive, he must fight to stay alive. We are also soldiers of the cross.

Not only that, but He has given us weapons to do it. These are not carnal, but mighty through God to pull down, demolish and destroy the strategies of the devil. There is a real devil. God created all things, even the devil. He has a job to do and he does it well. John 10:10 denotes his job description. "The thief cometh to kill, steal and destroy." Therefore our Lord controls all of his activity. He does nothing without the knowledge and permission of the Father.

Don't you know the devil is afraid of you? You should know that each morning you awaken and place your feet on the ground he trembles and questions God. He wants to know, "What is man that thou art mindful of him?" Though we are made a little lower than the angels, yet we have power over him and he does not like it. So he is at war with every believer because God has knowledge of us, and he loves us. Satan doesn't necessarily want us, he wants our souls and worship. And more so for us to curse God. As

Job's wife suggested to him, "Why don't you curse God and die." He is a liar and has already been defeated at Calvary. He has no teeth, he is now gumming it.

Aren't you glad to know his weapons are powerless against you? And that our weapons are not carnal, but mighty through God. The Christian walk is a fight. As long as we live in this body and seek to serve the Lord, we will need to learn how to contend after the Spirit. He teaches our hands to fight.

In Ephesians 6, Paul admonishes us to be always clothed with the whole armor of God. In this chapter the entire attire we should wear is outlined for us. Take heed that you are properly clothed. The Scripture reads, "Put on the whole armor," (meaning in its entirety).

- The helmet of Salvation: (a defense to your head and mind).
- The breastplate of righteousness: (protects the chest, primarily the heart).
- Your loins girded with truth: (middle and lower organs, includes sexual organs).
- Your feet shod with the preparation of the gospel (it is the beautiful feet that takes the gospel to the world).

- The shield of faith: (upper and lower body).

The greatest weapon we have is the Word within us.

It is God living on the inside of us, leading and directing us by the power of his Holy Spirit. He promises never to leave nor forsake us. The truth is, even as God was with the children of Israel as they went through the wilderness, He is the same with us as we go through our wilderness experience. On the other hand, if we stay in the Word, do our part, and see it as part of our destiny on the way to our final destination, we will find the struggles and pit falls we encounter along the way, not as devastating to us. But, God is able to give us the victory.

Again, these trials come to test our faith and love for him, this causes us to mature. They also make us better soldiers and contenders of the faith. They come to strengthen us in the power of His might and not ours. When the road gets rough and the going gets tough, He will always sustain us and under gird us with the right hand of His power. There is a war going on and it is taking place in the confines of our minds. Satan's intent is to pollute your heart. Don't allow your heart to be troubled. You have the ability to guard your heart with all diligence. The devil is roaming to-and-fro seeking whom he may devour. But

I tell you the truth, if we are grounded in the ways of God, he does not have a chance. For the Bible tells us, no weapon formed against us will prosper if we are cognizant of what we have. We have lethal weapons given unto us which are to be used against him. It is very important we possess this knowledge. It is obtained through knowing him. Not just knowing about him, but by maintaining a deep relationship with him.

To fight is to struggle, to be aggressive in competition. It is to contend with someone or something. And we know this relates to our adversary the devil. For the believer, this is not to be done in a worldly fashion, but after the spirit. "For though we live in the flesh we do not war after the flesh." If God says it we must do it. He promises that no weapon formed against us will prosper, or become effectual against us. We are more than conquerors through Christ. We are destined and designed to win every battle. He is our battle-ax, our shield, buckler, and high tower. He is a rock and fortress about us. We are garrisoned and compassed about with his love. The battle has already been won.

Know that your victory is in your praise. The song-writer puts it this way: "Breathe in His Name, and Breathe out a Praise, the fruit of your lips giving him praise."

Seek Wisdom:

We cannot put God in a box. We may not be scholars of the Bible, however that does not excuse us from being obedient. In gratitude we ought to be the best we can be for the Lord. As citizens of the Kingdom we are responsible for our own actions. Therefore we should always, seek to please God in all we do. This is so important. It is the reason most believers fail in their walk with him. We speak it, but in actuality we please ourselves and the circumstances surrounding us. The Lord becomes second place. Yet when we get in trouble we call on him. Oh but thank God, for his grace and mercy! Job discovered this when he said, "But, there is a spirit in man, and the inspiration of the Almighty causeth him to understand." (Job 32:8). This has become a favorite Scripture of mine. It assures me God is concerned with all of our ways, and he does respond when we call upon him for wisdom and understanding. Another translation refers to it as, "The breath of the Almighty gives him understanding."

Once while meditating in my quiet time with Him, I heard the Lord speaking to me through the Spirit. He called me by my name saying, "Gina, have you ever thought about using other tools?"

Immediately I knew it was not me thinking. I knew nothing about tools. Only the Holy Spirit could teach me this way. We limit God, though we have been given all things, other tools that pertain to life and godliness for us to use. Most of the time the only thing we can think about is the word or the Bible, these have become patent answers. Do we believe him? They are given to us to perfect and edify us, to prosper and make us whole. To help us grow in grace to the stature, and fullness of measure of Christ.

Other tools such as:

The Word, prayer, fasting and meditation. We also have access to these discipline gifts; ministry gifts, power of agreement with others, small groups or Bible study. Seminars, conferences, ministry in songs and the five-fold ministry; (Apostle, Prophet, Evangelist, Pastor and Teacher). These are only a few of the gifts we have to help us grow. Not counting all the brothers and sisters in the faith. It's good to know we don't have to walk this walk alone.

Most of the time we are programmed to think too small, so we don't explore other possibilities or alternatives given to us by God. We forget they are principles, precepts, statues, ordinances and commandments. There are also commands and laws. David in Psalms 119 often prayed that God would teach him and help him to keep them. There are other tools to strengthen us. We use the word of God so lightly without knowledge. It is one of the most powerful tools we have to help us prosper in the Kingdom. The kingdom of God is now, we must know its laws and principles in order to be successful. Yes, we will enjoy all we have been promised in the Eternal Kingdom. There won't be a need for us to believe for, healing, relationships, finances, food etc. because all will have been provided through redemption. We must understand its value in order for it to be profitable to us now.

It is not used in a consistent fashion by all. Sometimes even adding a little bit of common sense is wise. Especially if you feel you don't have enough knowledge of the Scriptures as others do. It may well be a lack of discipline in your study habits or a void of the Word perhaps coupled with the lack of faith on your part. Faith comes by hearing, and hearing by the Word. It is so important in these days for believers to begin to study the Word. Not just for church sake, but to be able to rightly divide it especially in times of trouble. The Bible states, "My people perish for lack of knowledge." Therefore, you may need to use your God- given-intuition by listening to the Holy Spirit to help some, until you get more of the Word in you.

Allow the Word to ground you and establish you in your ways. Therefore may I submit to you according to the Scriptures, the Word is sharper than any two edged-sword. It will correct the error in us every time. Also, if used improperly against a newborn believer, you could kill him or her prematurely before they have a chance to develop in their faith, and have the ability to handle themselves. Strong meat belongs to those who are mature. We must use wisdom and be led by the Spirit of God, and not by our own way when dealing with new believers.

You may say, "We have the Word of God, and must tell the truth. No one can refute it." I agree whole-heartedly. But to hold that viewpoint and not exercise sobriety may be injurious to others, especially a new believer. You may well be acting out of your flesh, and not wise in your discernment. This behavior could be a detriment to your spiritual growth in dealing with others, and being pleasing to the Father.

Demonstrating the Fruit of the Spirit:

Did you know that the greatest weapon against the devil is when you:

- Demonstrate the gifts and fruit of the Spirit?
- Be kind to one another, holding your peace

even when you don't feel like it or think you are correct.

- Be slow to anger and long-suffering. Love without seeing any wrong.
- Exhibit peace in the midst of stormy and chaotic moments when things become confusing.
- Be gentle with those whom you disagree with, and especially, to those you know don't like you.
- Be submissive when you know you have been ill-treated.
- Have a spirit of meekness though the devil tells you differently. Know that this may be interpreted as weakness, but remain steadfast. It is you demonstrating power under control, and willing to obey.
- Show temperance, it is a great virtue and gift or fruit of the Spirit. It keeps you balanced.

Weapons to fight with:

The greatest weapon we have against the devil is Intercessory Prayer, to do Spiritual Warfare. It is not pretty, passive or pious. We literally engage against the enemy in the Spirit. Are there bruises and scratches? Yes, but we have already won! Consider the case of the soldier who goes to war and wins, yet he sustains injury in the process. Or a boxer who receives a black eye and bloody nose during the match. Though he won the fight he has obvious battle scars. These are just a few illustrations amongst many others. I am persuaded that in every situation, favorable or unfavorable, if we approach it with a winning mentality, half of the battle will already be won. Therefore, the blows inflicted won't be as painful. Never begin with an attitude of defeat, but always maintain a victory mentality and attitude.

Transforming your mind (change):

"And be ye not conformed to this world, but be ye transformed by the renewing of your mind." (Romans 12:2) Our success depends on the way we perceive things. If we seek the will of God in everything He will make it known to us. On the other hand if we approach the battle or situation with a defeated attitude we have already lost. Having a winning mentality and experiencing victory requires a transformation of the mind through the Word and obedience. We cannot continue to think the same way and expect any kind of increase in any area of our life without a change. Recently, I heard a preacher make a quote saying, "Failure is not final, but failure to change may be fatal." I thought that was so profound, because if we continue to behave or think the same way, we will get the same results.

When and if we are in Christ, there ought to be some kind of noticeable change in us. We now do things differently because, our minds have been transformed. We have the mind of Christ. Change is evident whenever we are not conformed or molded into the ways of the world or our own thinking, but rather we submit to the leading of the Holy Spirit.

The Holy Spirit with us makes the difference in our thinking: This is the duty of the Holy Spirit (Parakletos). Jesus said in the book of John, "It is expedient that I go, and if I go I will send you another like myself." He promised not to leave us comfortless. He has sent the (Parakletos) comforter, to walk beside us. To lead and guide us into all truth. He, referring to (the Holy Spirit), is the one who keeps us on the straight and narrow path and in right standing with the Lord. He does it when we choose to obey Him not some of the time, but all of the time. We are not in this fight alone. Once we are saved, it will take a fight to remain saved. We know that it's grace that keeps us, as we also strive to do our part and experience a demonstrable change in our lives.

What does it mean to be transformed?

It means though not perfect, we strive to attain a level of obedience that pleases God. Not works of righteousness to warrant salvation, but good works that causes God to smile at your progress as you grow. We are in a constant fight from the moment we enlist in the army of God. You literally entered into warfare with the flesh and the Devil. Paul tells us to fight the good fight of faith; good because it makes us better, and because the good one is involved and goes before us each step of the way.

I can almost hear the cheer of the crowd of witnesses in Hebrews 12. On the side lines cheering us on, building us up in faith, as though saying, "Go Regina you can do it, keep the faith. As brother Joshua jumps in behind him saying, "Be of a good courage Regina, use the Word. Don't let it depart out of your mouth." And the cheer of many others echoing in the wind. These all obtained victory through their faith and perseverance as citizens of the Kingdom.

Every battle and situation is unique to each individual. It only prepares us for the next fight. Almost day by day, and throughout our walk with Christ we will encounter battles. Some more difficult than others. Nevertheless the good news is, we are not in this alone. We have Christ as our battle-ax. He is the captain of the host. He goes before us as our redeemer, defender and friend. The songwriter said, "There is not a friend like the lowly Jesus, no not one. No not one." I can almost feel the power in those words. It witnesses to my soul. He is that friend who sticks closer than a brother. He is a friend you can call upon anytime of the day or night. As humans we are always looking for someone to follow. There is no better choice you will ever make than to follow Jesus. In Him you will find a good relationship, friendship and fellowship. It hurts me to see people who so readily reject Christ and refuse to follow him. They find it so easy for them to say no to Him. Yet when it comes to Satan they do not seem to have any problem. Sometimes it is obvious they are suffering. Yet, they remain unrepentant through the struggle. I find it hard to comprehend why some people just utterly refuse to surrender to the ruler ship of Christ, when all he wants to do is to help them. He is the propitiation for sin, ordained by God, to bring us back to Him. There is no other means according to the Bible. Every person must come through Jesus, not through a religion, person, creed or way...!

As an evangelist and follower of Jesus, I seek every opportunity to snatch people out of the jaws of the enemy, whose only goal is to devour them. The devil does not like believers who witness for Christ. He especially hates those who understand their calling and duty as soldiers. The Bible tells us that the devil desires to kill, steal and destroy us. And more so, he is especially after those who seek to free others through the preaching of the gospel. One thing we must understand, and is worthy of repeating is that, though we walk in the flesh we do not fight or war in the flesh. We have powerful weapons given to us for warfare. Remember, it is only to be used against him, and not each other. They are not carnal, but mighty through God to pull down and destroy his tactics and works. There is not a weapon the devil has that is more powerful than the weapons of a believer who knows the Word of God. This concept is so vital to our endurance in the fight. The mind is the battlefield for the devil. None of us is exempt from his trickery. But, the newly converted believers are better prey because their defenses are undeveloped. They are yet babes in Christ. But thank God he always watches over us, and protects us from his brutal attacks. He causes us to be triumphant over all, or a new believer could fall and be severely damaged, before having an opportunity to bloom for Jesus. The Lord has also given us the power to cast down every evil and disruptive thought or attack on our minds. The enemy will try to replay our past to keep us in bondage.

Cut off every Evil Imagination:

How be it? We have the sword of the Spirit, which is, the Word of God. It is quick and powerful. It is thoroughly equipped and able to abolish every thought contrary to Gods Word. Understanding the power of the Word we possess in Christ, we have the ability to disarm him. We can dispossess him of his weapon and his ability to harm us or our loved ones. Literally render him impotent, useless, and good for nothing. Canceling every assignment or evil intention toward us.

Set your mind and intent

"No eye has seen, no ear has heard, no mind has conceive what God has prepared for those who love him." (1 Corinthian 2: 9 NIV)

We have no idea what things we can accomplish when we set our minds and intent to trust God. He knows those whose trust is in Him, who do not put their trust or confidence in the arm of flesh. It is a mindset and it changes our hearts. I believe exciting things are yet to be discovered. We have not even scratched the surface of the things God has in store for those who love him and serve him in righteousness.

A brief Testimony:

Recently I had a minor surgery of my knee and

was laid up in bed for a few days. It was the most amazing and evident transformation of my mind I had ever experienced. Unable to do anything else, I began to focus my attention on the Lord.

I remembered the pain I had with the previous surgery. So prior to surgery, I began to set my intent to trust God. This was not by any means foolish jesting, as a nurse I knew what to expect, and what I needed to do post operatively. Especially in regard to pain control. The importance of taking the medication after surgery to promote healing and prevent complications due to immobility. I knew I had poor tolerance to narcotics, though it helps the pain somewhat, it would also work adversely on my system. This is not to say I wouldn't take it after some other surgery. However, this time I opted not to.

I was aware of the pain because I previously had the same procedure done, I dreaded it badly. In prayer I asked the Lord to help me bear the pain, so I could avoid having to take any strong medication for those few days. It wasn't easy, however the Lord granted me the petition and I made it through. Not to say I didn't have any pain. Yes! I did. However I only took a few pills for only a couple of days, nothing like the first surgery, but I made it. Whenever the pain was too severe, I did everything to believe he would. I focused my mind on the scripture in Isaiah 53, which says, "He himself bore my infirmities and sufferings on the cross." I made sure I asked every one of my friends and church family, even those on the Gospel Conference Line, to pray for me and the pain. And I can truly say, I tried the Lord and he works. When the pain became intense I pressed into my Savior all the more. Like David, I cried unto the Lord and he heard me and delivered me from all my fears.

I was determined I was going to make it, and I did. As the days went by the Lord came through for me over and over again. You may say it was a silly thing to do. But I believe as I stepped out by faith in this little area, which to him is nothing but a light affliction. Later I will be able to trust him with greater things, even the healing of my eyes.

In 1979 the Lord gave me a promise concerning my vision, and I am yet standing on it. "The eyes of them that see shall not be dim," (paraphrase -Isaiah 32:3). This has kept me hopeful all this time. He often sends me reminders through other preachers as well.

Launch out into the deep:

He also reminded me of the promise of a great ministry. As I laid in bed one morning I had an unusual encounter with the Lord. It was calming to hear the voice of the Holy Spirit speaking to me through the Scriptures and while in prayer. This was different because He spoke to me about launching out into the deep by faith.

The amazing thing was, I tuned in to The Gospel Conference line just in time and heard the same subject mentioned. This was impacting to me more than ever. I knew the Lord was saying something. Not only had He visited me, but had deposited a word into my spirit as I was seeking Him earlier.

To hear a similar revelation on the subject was a confirmation. Though it was from a different perspective it did not conflict, rather it enhanced what I had received. It was so rich, my eyes were opened to some other things revealed to me. It was so refreshing all that day.

The message took me all the way back to a previous teaching I had done on Peter from the books of Matt, Mark, Luke 5:1-11 and John 21:1-6. It was so impressing I felt the Lord leading me in that direction. It is time for us to launch out into the deep with our faith. Be aware, the enemy will do everything he can to stop us. Everything we need is in the deep, but we need our minds transformed. The Good News is, the Lord confirmed his Word and many souls were saved healed and delivered. It was an awesome crusade in

Panama.

There is definitely a war going on, the Devil is a liar. We have read the end of the book. It says, "We win!" We are more than conquerors through Christ. I cannot help but to reaffirm that everything we need is in Christ. Without him we can do nothing. Neither are we anything against the devil or his emissaries, but with God! He is a defeated foe. . . . My God! Help us to know, what is in our hands.

Saints! The devil does not want you to know this, therefore having this bit of revelation may save you from his plot. You are powerful in Christ against his schemes. Even if it only manages to save an ear, or two legs from being devoured out of his mouth. "You could yet be profitable for the gospel. Like the Prophet Amos was able to do for the sheep." Amen! Fight your fight. Quit crying or you may be devoured. Sometimes as believers we whine and whimper too much. We get too caught up in our own issues, and we lose focus of the Father's business.

Micah 4 tells us that, "There is a King on the inside of us, and our counselor or coach has not perished." He says for us to quit crying, bear the pain, labor to bring forth as a woman in travail. (Paraphrased).aa

"Fight your fight!":

Fight from victory, not for victory. It is He who teaches your hands to fight. Fight not only for yourself, but for others also. You are saved to go save someone else. Break the bond of wickedness and set that captive free in Jesus name. Know your authority. Do not believe the lies of the devil. Some may say that this type of attitude is arrogance or presumption, not so. It is faith and confidence in The Lord Jesus.

Get rid of the Sin:

Get over the sin issue in your life, know for sure if you are saved. Jesus loves you. He died for you and wants to use you. He is depending on you to do greater things and exploits, for God's sake!

Too many believers are still dealing with sin in their life. They are still questioning whether or not they are saved. My advice to you is: "It's time you get over it," and begin to walk in dominion and Kingdom authority. Habitual sin causes you to live a defeated life. There is a job to be done by all of us. Souls are weighing in the balance and the devil is bidding high. My question is, "Who is on the Lord's side? Can you be counted on? Do you believe the report? Would you be willing to say I will go Lord, send me?" If you can't, you're probably not ready for the fight. Jesus says, if so you are not worthy to follow him. "And anyone who does not take their cross and follow me is not worthy of me." (Matthew 10:38). There is no time for religion and piety. We are living in the last days and perilous times are here. We see it in our communities and in the world. This is not gloom and doom. It is reality.

Jesus is now speaking expressly to the church. We must all take heed and do the work of an evangelist. The world needs to be reconciled and if it is to be done it will be through the entire body of Christ, not just by a few. Fight your fight! We have been ordained, or for a better word we have been prepared by God for this task. It is to go and show forth the praises of the Lord. Bring back the trophies for Jesus. We know that if we confess our sin, Jesus is faithful and just, to forgive us and cleanse us from unrighteousness. Not only some, but all. For all unrighteousness is sin. Jeremiah was told that God would forgive the wickedness of the children of Israel his chosen people and remove their sins from them. (Jeremiah 31:34). How much more will he do for a blood bought believer. The prophet puts it this way, "Where is another God like you, who pardons the sins of the survivors among his people? You will not remain angry, for you love to be merciful. Once again you will have compassion on us. You will tread our sins beneath your feet. You will throw them into the depths of the ocean. You will bless us as you promised Jacob long ago. You will set your love upon us, as you promised our father Abraham." (Micah 7:18 TLB) What more reassuring words than these do we need, though spoken to the children of Israel?

I appropriate this word to my life today, and so can you. It will definitely build your confidence in the God we serve. He is the same yesterday, today and will remain the same forever.

Be always watchful

We must always be on our guard as soldiers of the cross and of the Kingdom. As we watch for the devil he is also watching for us. He is cunning and crafty. We should also watch for sin as well as errors in our life. Examine our self-daily, giving no place to the devil. During one of my study sessions with the Lord I was meditating on the fight. I asked him, "What should I know about this fight I am in?" This is what came out of my spirit as I read the Scriptures. I believe it was from the Lord. He said for me to endure hardship as a good soldier. (2 Timothy 2:3) I looked up the word. I found it to mean the following:

• Purpose to live a life as a soldier, exposed to cold, heat, hunger, and strenuous exercise.

• Be a good leader.

• Be faithful to the call.

Endure: Kakopatheo: Be afflicted, suffer affliction or trouble, and endure hardness.

1 Peter 4:1 says, "Forasmuch then as Christ hath suffered for us in the flesh, arm yourselves likewise with the same mind. Christ knew no sin yet he suffered for us.

Watch: Nepho: When dealing with the devil you must be discreet. It means abstain, be sober and always watchful.

It also means to be strategic. He is cunning and crafty. The father of all lies, there is no truth in him.

Questions for discussion:

• Question: What are some of the myths you know about after you are saved?

• Question: What does Paul say about being a soldier?

• Question: Will you suffer as a Christian?

• Question: Will all of your struggles be over because you are born again?

I feel I would be amiss if I neglect to give you

the opportunity to say the sinner's prayer and invite Jesus into your heart as your personal savior and Lord.

The Bible says in Romans 10:9, 10, "That if thou shall confess with thy mouth the Lord Jesus, and shall believe in thine heart that God hath raised him from the dead, thou shall be saved. For with the heart man believeth unto righteousness; and with the mouth confession is made unto salvation." So if you believe the words you are about to pray, and will believe in your heart in truth, you will be born again today. Pray this prayer with me aloud:

Father I realize I am a sinner and I need a savior. I believe Jesus died for my sin and he rose from the dead. I now confess my sin and receive Jesus as my Lord and Savior and the only hope of a home in heaven. I now confess I have eternal life. Thank you Father for saving me. Thank you Jesus for coming into my heart. I promise to serve you and live for you the rest of my life Amen, and Amen.

Congratulations, if you believed what you just prayed, you are now part of the family. This means, by faith you are saved through the simplicity of the gospel. You may not have heard any bells ringing, or seen any flashing lights, but be assured you are now a citizen of the Kingdom, a Royal Priesthood. The angels in heaven are rejoicing over you at this very moment.

I thank you Lord, for all those who say this prayer in faith, believing. May you grant an abundant entry unto them into your Kingdom, and into your presence in Jesus name, Amen. Here are some words of encouragement from me to you now that you are in Christ. This is the most crucial moment after your decision to accept the Lord. You can, and must be confident of these:

You are now a part of the family of God. You have been given the righteousness of God in Christ Jesus. He is your Lord and Savior. You are now, more than a conqueror as well as an ambassador for Christ. (I mean as of this moment, move in that direction). You are now a soldier in the army of the Lord. You have all of the things you will need to live a godly life on the earth, which is through the Word. Greatness is now in you. It is Christ in you, the Hope of Glory. You have great and precious promises in the word from God your creator. It is the immutability of his word. He cannot lie or change. It cannot be broken, added to or taken away from. He will never leave you, neither will he forsake you. Keep your eyes and mind stayed on him and you will always remain in perfect peace. Know that the peace of God is worth more than your life in gold.

Do not forget, always be truthful and faithful

unto him and he will grant you divine favor in all you do. Also, divine favor will be granted everywhere you go according to his will for your life.

A few side notes: Notice I had no room for the sin issue that was in your life. Because I believe when you said the prayer it immediately was placed under the blood and washed away. Endeavor not to resurrect it. Render and consider yourself dead to it. Focus on the great things God wants you to accomplish and to accomplish through you. This should keep you busy and determined to reach your goal. You are now on the path of destiny. Keep your eyes and mind on the cross. Look to Jesus. Don't turn back, you have come too far. Don't give up your salvation and don't give in to the devil in the name of Jesus, Amen.

<hr>

Chapter 5

The Covenant: Like A Beautiful Tapestry

"For the law made nothing perfect, but the bringing in of a better hope did, by which we draw nigh unto God." (Hebrew 7:19).

"He predestined us to adoption as sons, through Jesus

Christ, to Himself, according to the kind intention of His will (Ephesians 1:5 NAS).

"But when the time had fully come, God sent forth his son, born of a woman, born under the law, to redeem those under law, that we might receive the full rights as sons." (Galatians 4:4, 5 NIV).

God is perfect in all of his ways. He will not make a mistake. It is said when we cannot track or trace his hands beloved, we can always trust his heart. I believe that! Our lives are like a beautiful tapestry weaved by the hands of God, and as intricate as it is, he will not miss a stitch. I heard an old hymn once which talked about the miracle of the "patch work" God is making of us. He's given us power to become sons. We as believers are his handy work.

It was in the eternal plan of The Father that we would be engrafted into his family as sons through adoption.

Adoption is so solid that in the old Roman law, a father could give up his own son, but by law it was not permissible to give up an adopted son. We have been adopted, we are twice His.

All of creation is waiting for us to manifest.

As we view the Scriptures we will see the

principle of the weaving of the covenant established from Genesis to Revelation. Jesus now being the mediator of this new covenant makes it better than that which was established before.

What is a Covenant?

Hebrew: berit (cutting) a transaction between God and man or man and his fellowman. A compact between man and man, ("allied"). (New Unger's dictionary) The ultimate talking dictionary defines it as: An agreement between God and man whereby God makes certain promises and expects certain behaviors of men in return. God makes this agreement signed with the blood of his only son, Jesus. It is not a contract which can be broken. It is immutable. After the Resurrection of Christ and through his shed blood, our relationship as believers became an intricate one. His will becomes ours, as well as ours his, because of the relationship we now share with him as priest. In John chapter 17 Jesus prayed to the Father, "That we may be one even as He and the Father are one." Throughout the Scriptures referring to the Old Testament, transcending into the New Testament, we are able to see the Weaving of the New Covenant. In the midst of the symbolism and metaphors used the portrayal of the Lord Jesus and Redemption surfaces. Allegorically speaking, I thought about the weaving process of a woman's hair. The real hair is mixed and hidden among the hair for weaving. (a picture of the Old and New Testament or law). The expectation is that it will substitute and produce a desired look, appearing as real, whenever the process is completed. As I mused on the Covenant and its implication to my life, I saw how God had so intricately weaved himself into the believer's life through Christ.

In the Old Testament we see Him always present with his people, and involved in every aspect of their lives. Desiring to dwell amongst them, He openly revealed himself to them at Calvary. His Grace and Mercy was manifested to humanity. There are various sophisticated methods of weaving used today. This makes it almost impossible to tell the difference between the real and the substitute. This is not to be offensive to anyone. It is how God chose to reveal this to me. He knows that I enjoy weaves, wigs, braids and all the rest of the vanity stuff. I am just being real. Since this tedious matter, the wig issue is clarified; perhaps we can go on. This is an area many women do not like talking about, bless God!

We are all familiar with the numerous terms used in regards to the Old and New Testament. Such as: The Old Testament concealed is the New

Testament revealed. It is also referred to as a preview of things to come. The Old is what was to come and the New Testament is when it came. The terminology used does not matter. Nevertheless, it is imperative that we have an understanding of what the Covenant is. How it originated, how it relates to us as believers and as heirs of the promise, and of the Kingdom. Thank God he has chosen us to enter into a blood covenant relationship with Him. He himself instituted the system and accepted the temporary offering as a shadow of what was to come. He knew they could not totally keep the commandments so their belief was accounted unto them as righteousness, and the wrath of God was satisfied. Now we are made righteous through redemption and by the washing and cleansing of the blood of Jesus, through faith. Hallelujah, glory to God. We are now accepted in the beloved. It was the Lord Jesus who suffered and died for our sins that now we may live unto God in righteousness.

The Old Testament is not just a series of events or rituals. Neither is it about genealogy, history or for reading sake. It is that we might believe that Jesus is the Christ, the Son of the Living God. By believing we might have hope through his name as the Scriptures points out. "For everything that was written in the past, was written to us, so that through endurance and the encouragement of the Scriptures we might have hope." (Romans 15:4). Through it we learn the character and mode of operation of our Lord in the past, and how he deals with us today through grace. He is the same yesterday, today, and forever.

The covenant serves to bring us into a right relationship with our creator, the Lord who was, and is and is to come. So that by our relationship to Him, we might be transformed into his image. The more we allow Christ to be formed in us, the more we are changed. The more we will grow up unto the fullness of the stature and measure of Christ, enabling us to be partakers of His Divine nature as heirs and joint heirs with Christ. We can see the portrayal or a picture of the ultimate sacrifice of Jesus the Christ,(as the tapestry) weaved in through the practice of the sacrificing of bulls, goats and other animals. This was only a temporary system until Christ. (Atonement).

Just imagine the amount of blood by bullocks and goats and other animals it took to satisfy the wrath of God on a yearly basis. Compared to the blood of one man Jesus once and for all.

This system was temporarily instituted by God for sin, to satisfy his wrath. It allowed his children to come into his presence each year through the blood of animals. The Bible says without the shedding of blood, there is no remission of sin. It was to be the means whereby they could offer up their sacrifice and worship.

Meaning they had to come willingly and offer up a sacrifice, a sin offering unto the Lord. (Read Exodus 21:16-18). Thank God today he chooses us, though we have the right to reject the call. We also must respond willingly. "If any man hear my voice and ask me to come in, I will come in and supp with him, and he with Me." (paraphrase Revelation 3:20)

I certainly consider this more than ever a Genesis moment in this season of my life. A new beginning and time where God is tearing down everything that is contrary to his Word. Doctrines, traditions and sayings picked up on the way to my destiny. At the beginning I found some things difficult and painful to release. Then I thought of what I would gain by doing so. The peace and intimate fellowship with Him. I recognize most things were religious in nature and had to be burned out of me. They were not doctrinally sound and God could not honor them, no matter how I prayed or fasted. I realized he will not alter any of his word for any of us. They weren't big things, nevertheless some were hindrances to my growth. Sometimes it is difficult to put in words our interaction with the Lord in our quiet times. Yes, I do believe the Lord is still speaking expressly, and he is very specific about what he desires for us to do. As you read the Word, it will be made clear. The Spirit impressed upon my heart as saying, "I am not indebted to honor sayings but the truth of my word only." Willfully and with much prayer I surrendered them all. You will be surprised at the things we hear in meditation, and in the secret place with him. He unlocks the deep secrets of our hearts and will show it to us if we allow him. Each individual is responsible to examine their own relationship and faith as well. Even as we are admonished to do, to see whether we are in the faith.

Having to re-do my thinking was not easy, but it was well worth it. Romans 12:2 says, "Be ye not conformed to this world but be ye transformed by the renewing of your mind. This phrase 'be ye' places a great responsibility on the individual believer to be accountable for his or her own beliefs and understanding of God's word. It is an action word and it is continuous. Likewise it is a command and not an option. When you discover that something does not line up with the Word of God, get rid of it, repent, and seek the Lord for clarity. Often times we put it on the back shelf to do later. Know that if transformation is to take place, you must be diligent about this matter, now. There are battles to be won. Victories to be attained and souls to be gained for the Glory of God.

In Ephesians 1:18 Paul prayed, "That the eyes of your understanding would be enlightened that you would know what is the hope of your calling and what is the inheritance as a saint in light. When your eyes are opened your thinking will be changed because now you see through the eyes of God, and possess the mind of Christ. We can no longer walk in darkness or remain in slumber. There is an expectancy of the Lord for every believer who professes Christ.

I knew I was experiencing a transformation when I felt as though God was requiring a more explicit and defined understanding of the Word from me. Because of it, I began to study more. There was a hunger and stirring in me for the Word. The curiosity in my heart on certain issues increased. I found myself seeking more and more answers. I was surprised, nevertheless I told Him yes! I will obey. I will seek to know you better in the power of your resurrection and in the fellowship of your suffering. Believe me it has been a journey.

Shortly thereafter the Lord began to deal with me about writing the book, *If I Never See Another Sunshine I Will Still Love God.* I was not at all ignorant of the Devil's devices to deceive me and to keep me mediocre in my faith. He thought he could keep me worrying and blinded from the truth. I fought to tear down every false ideation and lie he told me concerning my vision. It only made me seek the Lord more, he should've left things alone. In this book, I shared some of the things which God dealt with me about and how I made a conscious decision to walk in the blessing of my covenant rights. I'm finding many interesting, yet challenging moments in this new season. They keep me praying.

Sometimes I hear the term used in Christian circles: "Beyond or behind the veil". Though this is for my own clarity. The Scriptures plainly teach us, the veil has been rend in twain at the resurrection of the Lord Jesus Christ.

We can now come boldly before the throne of God as a priest with unveiled and open face. Thank God, I'm now able to behold my Redeemer as we commune through the Word in awe and reverence because of the righteousness of Christ. We sing, "Oh the wonder of it all" to the one who brought change to the world through his death. The Lamb of God slain before the foundation of the world. He shall be called wonderful, Counselor, and Mighty God the Scriptures reveal. I thank God for that place called Mount Calvary, and I thank Him for that old rugged Cross. Had it not been for it my soul would be lost. The other day I heard an old familiar song, my soul was blessed.

He had to go to Calvary, it was for my change and your change. The sacrifice of bulls and doves could not do it, but Jesus came and redeemed us. He paid the ultimate price. His sacrifice obtained for us a better covenant and partnership with God.

Prayer: Father I thank you so much, for you saw fit to invite me into partnership with you. Jesus, with your blood you made my salvation possible. Thank you for making my heart your dwelling place. I am forever grateful for the cross. Lord open my mind that it might be receptive to your truths. Reveal to us the significance of knowing you in a deeper way. Allow us dear Lord to exit the place of always confessing, but never experience what it is to possess because of our preconceived and deceptive thoughts. Dear God let every man, every devil, tradition, ideation and self-taught philosophy be a liar, but let God be real. In the name of our Lord and Savior Amen.

Chapter 6

The Cross Made A Difference

All of us have failed at one time or another because of sin. The reasons are endless, and too varied to even try to define. Nevertheless God has a solution. These are situations I have personally encountered throughout the ministry, in family and friends. Don't worry I found a few tucked away in me, but I have long-since taken care of them. Glory to God!

Here are some suggested reasons I believe may be some of the problem:

• Lack of knowledge

• Rebellion, and pride

• Upbringings, generational curses Childhood vows and bitter root judgments made

• Disappointments and damaged emotions.

• Unforgiven and unconfessed sins.

• Issues of the heart of man

I believe the condition of the heart is one of the primary reasons for failure to serve God in Spirit and truth. Unless we acknowledge the problems in our heart, we will be fighting a losing battle. "The heart is desperately wicked. Who can know it?" the Bible says.

Secondly we must have a desire to change. No one can make us do anything we have not first, purposed to do in our heart.

The reason is not as important as is the desire to change. The apostle Paul reminded the brethren saying they would be saved if they believe the preaching of the gospel, and by faith, stand firm on the word. (1 Corinthians 15:1 Paraphrased)

After salvation we will be better able to correct the behavior or problem through the power of the Holy Ghost given to us. As we grow in knowledge there is a transformation that takes place in our minds, whereby we are no longer conformed or in bondage to the circumstances in life, through faith and obedience. It is a continuing process. Without our involvement, it will not go away overnight because we are now saved. No matter what the circumstance, it's OK! God has given us a way out. I heard one of my pastors use this quote saying: "Failure is not final, but failure to change may be fatal." How great a truth to bear in mind.

There appears to be a sense of disregard and

resistance to change today in some churches. It's on the job, in society, in our schools, government, and even in our homes. Notice I started with the church, those who profess to be in Christ. There is no excuse for the believer. We have a responsibility to govern our lives accordingly because of the Word living inside of us. It is our manual, and it contains the protocol for godly living.

According to Galatians 5:16, 22-25, we are commanded to walk in the Spirit and we (shall) not gratify or fulfill the lust of the flesh. I like the 'shall not's of God. This is a command with a promise of fulfillment to those who do it.

If we confess or acknowledge ourselves to be followers of Christ, it is expedient we crucify the flesh daily, nailing it to the cross. If we allow the Holy Spirit to be our guide and counselor, we will grow in the Spirit and we will be kept by the power of God. We won't be in any way unfruitful.

In His image:

From the beginning we were created according to the image and likeness of God. Meaning we possess his Divine nature on the inside. Not only do we have the written word, but the Living word as well. It is Christ living in us.

He is our example and the express image of God the Father. Because of the promises given unto us we are now become partakers of his divine nature, by those same promises. By interpretation, meaning we have his character carved out on the inside of our being.

Trials and Temptations:

"That the trial of your faith, being much more precious than gold that perisheth, though it be tried with fire, might be found unto praise and honor and glory at the appearing of Jesus Christ." (1 Peter 1:7).

"Beloved, think it not strange concerning the fiery trial which is to try you, as though something strange happened unto you." (1 Peter 4:12).

Jesus Christ was tempted at the hand of Satan, in a greater way once and for all for us, so that we wouldn't have to. He got us victory over it, as narrated in the book of Matthew chapter 4. Therefore, know that your faith is tried by fire, to God it is much more precious than gold. I believe because we were made in His image and have His Divine nature, DNA, he seeks to find Himself in us. And to see whether we are maturing, according to the fullness of the measure and stature of Christ and to reward you after, if you endure the test. God tempts no man. Every temptation comes either from the devil or the lust of the flesh. God will use that temptation to try your faith. Temptation comes to every man and will prevail if he allows himself to be is drawn away by his own lust, according to James chapter 12:1-14.

In spite of the trials, God still require for us to maintain godly standards.

It is not a pass or fail, but it is because of his love. It seems as though in the midst of it, He gives us a pop quiz and examines our heart in order to bring us up to par, (a state of being essentially equal or the equivalent with Jesus). According to James 1, we are blessed. We are perfected through the trials. The intent is to use us for the purpose of furthering the gospel. And by us exhibiting his divine nature, sinful men will be drawn to the cross.

Imperfect Vessels:

The prophet Jeremiah was once cited by the Lord to go down to the potter's house. He wanted to speak to him there. The remembrance of this encounter is worthy of provoking us to have our minds transformed. We will then understand our purpose in God. Who we are in His hands, and what he wants to do in us. We need to know who we are in the Lord. Our desire should be to fulfill the plans He has for us. Each time I read this passage I say to God, "Lord make me over again. You are the potter I am the clay. Make me, mold me, fill me, and then Lord use me for your glory."

Priests unto God:

Our eyes haven't seen and our ears haven't heard the things our Father has in store for us as his children. In the book of Exodus 19: 5, God gave Moses a message for His people saying, "Now if you obey me fully and keep my covenant, then out of all nations you will be my treasured possession. Although the whole earth is mine, you will be for me a Kingdom of priests and a holy nation." These same promises transcends to us today through Christ. We are partakers of a better covenant.

"But you are a chosen people, a royal priesthood, a holy nation (1 Peter 2:9).

Hearing the voice of God:

"Knowing this first that no prophecy of the scripture is of any private interpretation. For the prophecy came not in old time by the will of man: but holy men of God spake as they were moved by the Holy Ghost." (2 Peter 1:20, 21).

First of all I want to point out that a revelation:

is that which has been revealed or made known. It is what God shows you through whatever mode he desires to do it, such as dream, vision, and a word from others, through the Scriptures, etc. However, if it is of God it is divinely imparted through the Spirit and that no one can take away or refute that it wasn't God but God himself.

No individual has the ISBN, Copyright, Patent or ownership of any kind on the Bible. The bible was divinely written as holy men of God wrote under the inspiration of the Holy Spirit. Be very careful, your revelation shouldn't contradict or be in conflict with the Word. It's not God if it is not supported by the Scriptures.

Does it sound like God?

As believers we should know what sounds like God and what doesn't. However, it should always be based on the word. We may hear some things, which we know aren't scriptural. Be very careful what things we entertain as truth. The Bible fore-warns us to try the spirits, see whether they are of God. It may sound eloquent, but may not be necessarily scriptural in its content.

Many times, I would hear the same verse of Scripture repeated in diver's places. Usually my first perception is: "The Holy Spirit is attempting to say something to me", (the law of double reference). It could be that I was not hearing something he wanted me to do. You cannot and will not do what you don't hear. Though some people hear and yet they don't do.

Many people miss God and do not experience any substantial change or evidence of consistency because of their inability to hear him. We all can say Amen to this.

It is written, "He that hath an ear, let him hear what the Spirit is saying." The Lord is always speaking.

In order to change, it is necessary for us to hear. "For faith cometh by hearing, and hearing by the word of God." We cannot do what we haven't heard, or could it be we have heard, but refuse to do.

Lately, more than usual I feel the Lord making me more sensitive to his voice.

Recently I've experienced God trying to get my attention. For over a week I was reluctant to respond to the small voice inside. Each time I wiped the kitchen counters something seemed to say to me, (the Holy Spirit) "Move the microwave and wipe behind it." I continued to ignore the voice. Actually I set a day that I would do it. Finally after being constantly bombarded by the thought, I decided I would move it. To my amazement that morning when I moved the microwave, I discovered that a banana had fallen behind it and had rottened. It had to have been there for a few weeks at least.

I realized that had I recognized the voice, I would've obeyed sooner. There have been numerous other occasions of this same sort. Each day, I'm learning how to listen and be more mindful of the small voices on the inside.

Is it Worship?

The prophet Isaiah noticed the people worshipped with their lips and not from the heart. The more I minister, the more I realize it is possible for people to worship without knowing who they are worshipping and not procuring that it is Spirit and in truth. Jesus told the woman at the well in John 4:22a, "Ye worship ye know not what: we know what we worship." Some may get offended whenever one touches this area. They would say things like, "We cannot judge how people worship, we all have our own way, and God understands." Yes we don't know the heart, but the Bible is clear in its teachings on worship. And it can be characterized by what we see. It is something we do not have to defend. He does not want religious rituals, but true worship. He deserves it. There is a way that seems right, which ends in death according to the Word. In fact Jesus made it clear to the disciples saying, "Do not be offended at my words." He desires for us to worship Him in Spirit and in Truth.

David also spoke saying in Psalm 119:165, "Great peace have they which love my law and nothing shall offend them. It ought to be a delight to show your worship." It exalts the Lord. We should always examine our hearts to see our response. If it offends us, correct it, you have a problem.

Issues of the Heart:

"A good man out of the good treasure of his heart bringeth forth that which is good: and an evil man out the evil treasure of his heart bringeth forth that which is evil: for of the abundance of his hearth his mouth speaketh." (Luke 6:45)

It is of utmost important for us to be honest, not only with God, but also with ourselves. He wants us to open up to Him and share our heart as children. After all He already knows what's in it. He won't kill us for being honest. The prophet Isaiah declared that the people worshipped God with their lips, but their hearts were far from Him. Know what is in your heart. Every word you speak comes from the words you have in you. Good or bad. No one can bring anything out of you that is not already in there. We sometimes blame circumstances or others, of which neither is at fault. We fail to understand the problem is coming directly from our heart. Whatever comes out of the heart influences your behavior because your flesh is ruling.

As a man or woman thinks in their heart, so are they. Your heart is the core part of your being and we are commanded to guard it from anything evil entering in. This will corrupt your thinking and cause issues later that you cannot justify. The key is to examine our heart and keep short accounts. Repent when necessary before your heart is hardened. Nevertheless God is able to take away the stony heart and give you a heart of flesh according to Ezekiel 36:26.

The heart of man is evil and desperately wicked. God is not alarmed because of this evilness. This should be a great consolation to know. Not only can He replace the heart, but He can also put a right Spirit in you. This will cause you to walk according to his statutes and commandments.

David was a man after God's own heart. He asked the Lord to renew a right Spirit within him, with repentance and acknowledgement of his sin at Psalm

51. He will do the same for us if we repent.

1 John 1:9 says, "If we confess our sins, he is faithful and just to forgive us of our sin and to cleanse us from all unrighteousness.

"Anyone who listens to the word and does not do what it says is like a man who looks at his face in a mirror and after looking at himself, immediately goes away and forgets what he looks like" (James 1:23, 24). He then experiences a mistake in identity because he lost sight of the image of God in which he was created.

We cannot fix our own problems, but if we know the reason for our behavior and are convicted to change. Instead of covering it up, we should expose it and allow God to show us ourselves. Then we won't be like that man looking in the mirror, seeing what he ought to be like, then turns away and he forgets what manner of man he is. He has actually lost his identity by not staying focused on Christ who is the author and finisher. He is our example, our guide, the one whom we are supposed to follow.

God desires obedience, and will bring healing and deliverance to our lives if we cry out to him.

As humans we seldom want to hear what we are doing wrong.

However, God has given us the five-fold ministry gift to perfect the body. To get us ready for his return.

These functions are as follow:

A. The Apostle the thumb finger, (governs).
B. The Prophet, the pointer finger (guides) receives a direct word and points us to what thus says the Lord.
C. The Evangelist the tallest, middle finger (gathers) as in outreach.
D. The Pastor, ring finger, a man after God's own heart, (guards).
E. The Teacher, the pinky finger (grounds) in the Word. The Devil, the accuser of the brethren recognizes their apostolic duty so he uses subtle tactics to deceive them in their hearts. Therefore whenever these issues are dealt with they are perceived as judging or condemning. He uses these tactics to intimidate and shut us up. To keep the people from repenting. However, a true witness who is called is bold as a lion and is not afraid to speak out, but stands on the word and proclaims it in faith.

Prayer: Holy Spirit thank you for your convicting power to make us know when we are doing right, and showing us the love of the Father. Thank you for searching our hearts. Cause us to repent. Take away that stony rebellious heart and give us a heart of flesh that we may serve God better. Thank you for the transforming power of the Word. In the name of Jesus the Christ Amen!

About the Author

Evangelist Thomas is an ordained minister of the Gospel. The Founder of Restorative Hope Ministry Inc. since the year 2000, and of The Panama Mission Campaign an outreach ministry to Panama and Mexico, She is also the founder of (Mujeres de Proposito Intl. Panama). Author of the books:

• "Walking by Faith Swaddled In His Glory." Translated in to the Spanish version: • "Caminando Por Fe Fajado en Su Gloria" • "If I Never See Sunshine I will Still Love God" • "Transforming Grace Calvary"

Her motto is: "Reaching the lost at any cost until all have heard". And "Whatsoever is born of God overcomes the world". In spite of her visual impairment Regina lives a full and busy life for the Lord. She is available to share her experiences.

Regina D. Thomas

CONTACT ME:
treginapma@aol.com
Visit me at:
www.restorativehopeministry.org
www.youtube.com/panamamission.com
www.youtube.com/panamamissioncampaign

803-834 3341

www.ingramcontent.com/pod-product-compliance
Lightning Source LLC
Chambersburg PA
CBHW031516040426
42445CB00009B/256